W9-BMU-387

Advance Praise For The
NEW EDITION OF TRACKS IN THE STRAW

"Ted Loder has done it again — taken ordinary images we bypass every day and woven them into creative Advent/Christmas stories radiant with sneaky tracks of divine mystery. This book is a remarkable invitation to a profound pilgrimage."

— *The Rev. Dr. W. Paul Jones, Professor Emeritus, Saint Paul School of Theology, Author of Theological Worlds: Understanding the Alternative Rhythms of Christian Belief*

"The splendid new stories in the Revised Edition of *Tracks in the Straw* are deep and intriguing, and draw us toward a fresh experience of the nativity through the eyes of unlikely participants in the first Christmas. The new personal prologue and epilogue reveal Ted Loder's keen eye for holy mystery, and I'd buy a new copy just for those! The new arrangement, with readings for each day in Advent, makes this book a read-aloud antidote for the crazy commercialism of the season."

— *Marjory Zoet Bankson, President, Faith at Work*

"Ted Loder has again made 'tracks' across the minds and souls of all of us who search for meaning in our lives. His personal reflections and honest questioning mirror our own struggles. *Tracks in the Straw* is his Christmas gift to a world facing an uncertain future. This book gives fresh 'birth to God's Spirit!' "

— *Dr. Bob Edgar, President, Claremont School of Theology; Former member of the United States House of Representatives*

"*Tracks in the Straw* is brilliantly and compassionately written. It tells 'the old story differently,' in vivid and engaging ways, powerfully demonstrating the Advent experience in the lives of real people in real situations. It is a MUST-READ for all who long to experience Christmas in a rich, new way. You'll not only want to read the stories this Christmas season but every Christmas to come."

— *Mary Scullion, RSM, Co-founder, Project H.O.M.E., Philadelphia*

Praise for Ted Loder's Books

Guerrillas of Grace

"An embarrassingly beautiful collection of prayers." — *Dr. William Muehl, Yale Divinity School*

"These prayers liberate the imagination to new experiences of God, grace and the stuff of life." — *Sojourners*

"Fresh, provocative, outrageous, funny, agonizing . . . always poetic, often prophetic." — *Rev. Robert Raines*

"One of the best such collections I have ever read . . . a poet who articulates for us what we long to say." — *Bishop Forrest C. Stith, Bishop of the New York West Area of the United Methodist Church*

Wrestling the Light

"If you haven't discovered the literary contributions of this preacher/prophet/poet/storyteller, let this new book be your joy . . . there's more grace in his poems and stories than in all the sweet talk about Jesus in America." — *Circuit Rider*

"Ted Loder gives expression to our human struggle to meet God in our living and our dying . . . he touches what is most human in himself and invites us to find grace along with him." — *Dr. Herbert R. Reinelt, Professor of Philosophy, University of the Pacific*

"A robust book that will enrich anyone who wants an authentic word of faith in today's world . . . catapults us past the surface to the wonder and mystery of God's grace." — *Rev. Dr. Arvin R. Luchs, Conference Council Director, Oregon-Idaho Annual Conference, The United Methodist Church*

"A conversation with God that fills the heart, exposes the insecurities, and renews the spirit . . . sheds the usual saccharin certainties and makes God the very bread of life." — *Dr. Caryn McTighe Musil, Feminist Educator, National Fellow, Association of American Colleges*

"A breath-taking peep at a grace-filled, high spirited God . . . Loder fans will not be disappointed!" — *Faith at Work Magazine*

Additional Praise for Ted Loder

"Creative imagination is rare enough in our time, and when it appears under literary and theological discipline in a preacher, it is cause for celebration. Ted Loder brings his phenomenal gifts to ancient biblical stories, and in his lyrical, penetrating retelling of them we confront ourselves." — *Dr. B. Davie Napier, Professor Emeritus, Yale University; President Emeritus, Pacific School of Religion*

"To read Ted Loder is to hear a different drummer, a different tune . . . his prose is poetry. He hears what we strive so hard to hear: the inner meanings, the truth about ourselves and our relationships." — *Dr. William F. Fore, Executive Director, Communication Commission, National Council of Churches*

"A creative and prophetic poet who will not stay in the pulpit." — *Dr. W. Paul Jones, Professor Emeritus, Saint Paul School of Theology*

Tracks in the Straw
Tales Spun from the Manger
REVISED EDITION

Ted Loder

Augsburg Books

TRACKS IN THE STRAW
Tales Spun from the Manger

First Augsburg Books edition © 2005. Copyright © 1985, 1997 Innisfree Press, Inc., Philadelphia, Pennsylvania, International Copyright secured. All rights reserved. Printed and bound in the United States.

Large-quantity purchases or custom editions of this book are available at a discount from the publisher. For more information, contact the sales department at Augsburg Fortress, Publishers, 1-800-328-4648, or write to: Sales Director, Augsburg Fortress, Publishers, P. O. Box 1209, Minneapolis, MN 55440-1209.

ISBN 0-8066-9014-3

The paper used in this publication meets the minimum requirements of American National Standard for Information Sciences—Permanence of Paper for Printed Library Materials, ANSI Z329.48-1984. ♾ ™

Manufactured in the U.S.A.

09   08   07   06   05   3   4   5   6   7   8   9   10

Contents

Introduction   **7**

A Personal Prologue: "I Feel Better"   **12**

In The Shadows

Clumsy Beautiful   **20**

The Ninth Woman   **25**

Eyelight   **28**

Tangled in a Line   **32**

Under Their Noses   **36**

Way Over Our Heads

Naked Isn't the Last Straw   **42**

We Can Tell You A Secret

The Thwig Eater   **58**

Tickled from Behind   **67**

Trillia Minor   **75**

That Strangest Of Nights

A Twist of Hospitality   **84**

When the Shavings Sing   **96**

A Wide Berth   **116**

And Now . . .

Gum on the Altar   **146**

A Personal Epilogue: "Christmas in the Ruins"   **170**

For Mark, David, Karen, and Thomas
whose stories are wondrous
and whose tracks are in my heart.

Introduction

Start with the visit of the angel Gabriel to the peasant girl Mary. Most of us have heard the story so many times we glaze over whenever we hear it yet again, if indeed we pay much attention to the Christmas story at all. But I risk beginning with this visit because it takes us quickly to the heart of the mystery of Advent/ Christmas and the why of this book. Gabriel comes to Mary and says, "Greetings, favored one. The Lord is with you."

What's Mary's reaction? "She was much perplexed by his words and wondered what sort of greeting this might be."

What's so striking is that this exchange between Gabriel and Mary happens *before* there is any word to Mary about her becoming pregnant by the Holy Spirit, about her bearing and giving birth to the Messiah. All Gabriel says is, "God favors you. God is with you," and Mary is in a dither of confusion.

Why? Of all the possible reasons, cut to the main one. Mary is confused because if God is with her, why can't she see him, touch him? If God favors her, loves her, where is he?

That is the core issue of Christmas, if not of religion itself. If God is real, why isn't God as evident to us as everything else that's real?

Mary's confusion gets worse when she learns she is to become pregnant and give birth to the Messiah even though she's a virgin. "How can this be?" she asks. She's told it will happen by the activity of God. The invisible God of all creation will become visible in a human being. That doesn't clear up the mystery, it just deepens it. So Mary says all anyone could say: "Let it be with me according to your word."

God pitching his tent in human history and our personal histories? The Spirit that hovered over the deep darkness at creation becoming flesh to live among us? Indeed, "How can this be?" If God is real, if God is with us, if God loves us, where is she? Why can't we see him, hear him? So our struggle is very like Mary's. In a way it is even more complicated because, for us in our technological age, mystery is considered to be something we don't know *yet* rather than something that is essentially unknowable. We are proudly resistant to Mary's trusting reaction, "Let it be with me according to your word."

We insist we're not intellectually naive and admit we're not pure or virginal — spiritually or otherwise — so our questions take a different shape but are just as compelling as Mary's. How can God be with us in the common reality of our daily lives, our confusion, our struggle, our poverty and pain, our small hopes and little loves? How can there be anything like birth, or rebirth, or new life in us or through us?

Still, the drama begins: "Greetings, favored ones. The Lord is with you." There it is, the heart of Advent, of Christmas . . . and the heart of our confusion. Augustine wrote of the mystery of the incarnation by concluding it was the visible disclosure of an invisible reality. Obviously, something visible cannot fully reveal what is invisible. It can only point to that invisible reality. It cannot reduce it to visible proportion or prove it by measurable data. So why doesn't God make things more plain? I believe it's a matter of grace.

One cold night about a year ago, I sat with a man on his patio.

The man had just tragically lost his beloved young wife, mother of three children, eleven-, nine- and six-years old. We struggled and stammered together to try to understand what such a loss meant, how God could let it happen, where God was in the face of this enormous pain. Recently I heard from that man. He wrote, "I will never forget that night on my patio and the way you said, 'This is why God hid Moses in the cleft of the rock: we can't live looking at God full in the face.'"

I remember that night, too, and I know that no one can look at the face of God and live. It would be too much for any of us to see such utter incomprehensible holiness and glory and power. There is something terrible as well as tender about God. So God put Moses in the cleft of a rock and kept his hand over the cleft until he passed, and then he let Moses see only his backside — a trace, a glimmer.

Yes, it's a story, but absolutely true and resonant as well with the deeper mystery of Advent/Christmas. We are all in some kind of cleft: a cleft of time and space, a cleft of culture, family, humanity: a cleft of our mortality, our finitude. There are things we cannot see, or touch. They remain invisible.

Even so, we can see glimpses, glimmers of the invisible, terrible, tender God in the incarnation, profoundly true glimmers but necessarily incomplete. The glimpses are heartening, healing, compelling, yet confusing, and they arouse the imagination. It cannot be otherwise with great, unfolding truth. Or with the mystery of God. As the gospel of John affirms in one breath, "The Word became flesh . . ." yet cautions in the next, "No one has seen God."

So we come face-to-face with the real mystery of Advent/Christmas. God is not just somewhere "back there" or "out there" but "right here." As I said in the introduction to the First Edition of *Tracks in the Straw*, that means the mystery is a very human one.

And yet, what makes the human mysterious is the presence of God in it, with us. So the human story is really always about God and what God does with, in, and for human beings in spite of ourselves.

For the mystery of Advent/Christmas is the mystery of the human and the specific — as specific and human as each one of us, as the face you saw in the mirror this morning, as the old woman you passed on the stairs, as the children you almost tripped over on your way out of the subway or into the office, as the shoppers elbowing their way through to the store counters, as the human faces and shapes and sizes and colors wandering the streets with you.

I titled this book *Tracks in the Straw* to suggest that God isn't obvious in entering the world. What is more ordinary than a baby's birth to a poor family in a poor country? Still, God leaves "tracks" in the straw. The tracks are faint but there for those who look and follow them with imagination. And imagination is the dancing partner of faith.

Poet Kathleen Norris writes that in Ephesians when Paul explicitly compares marriage with Christ's love for the church, he finally gives up and simply says, with exasperation as well as wonder in his voice, "This is a great mystery." Norris concludes, this is "what happens when you discover a metaphor so elusive you know it must be true. As you elaborate, and try to explain, you begin to stumble over words and their meanings. The literal takes hold, the unity and the beauty flee. Finally you have to say, I don't know what it means; *here it is.*"[*]

The poet's insight holds for the birth of Jesus and what it means, and for the Advent/Christmas season that gathers around it. Though that birth is surely not just a metaphor, it is a mystery because it involves the unknowable — dare I say sneaky? — ways of God.

* *The Cloister Walk*, Kathleen Norris, Riverhead Books, New York, 1996.

I put my experience of that incredible mystery in stories because I believe with all my heart that is the most accurate and faithful way to follow God's tracks in the straw. I have rewritten the stories from the First Edition of *Tracks in the Straw*, some radically, some moderately, so they will carry more powerfully the awe and the possibilities of Christmas. I have added some new stories and omitted others. The stories also have been arranged so that they can be read one section each day of Advent.

I have tried to add something deeper to the book as I have gone deeper into my own experience of the mystery of Christmas and my reflections on what it means. These stories are for everyone who knows the ache and insistence of longing in their lives — believers, doubters, clergy, laity, families, single people, old, young, black, white, brown, male, female, you.

Now, after stumbling over words and their meaning, yet trusting that the terrible, delightful, healing wonder and beauty has not fled them, and thanking those whose feedback has helped me with this new edition, most especially my beloved wife, Dr. Jan Filing, as well as my gifted colleague, Dr. Ann Marie Donohue, and my remarkable editor, Marcia Broucek, I say with exasperation and wonder at what I have written: "I don't know all that it means. *Here it is!*"

A Personal Prologue

"I Feel Better"

Every chance he gets, which is too often, a friend of mine says, "It's the end of the world as we know it, and I feel fine." He swears the saying is original, but I'm sure he picked it up somewhere. At first I chuckled when he said it, now I roll my eyes. I know if it really was the end of the world as he knows it, he wouldn't feel so fine.

At least I know I wasn't feeling fine that night three days before Christmas as I drove through the rain and sleet to meet my daughter Karen for a late supper at a center city tavern she liked. The world I knew was ending, not just in the somewhat abstract way it always is, but very specifically and painfully.

Karen, my bright, beautiful kid, had dropped out of college to try to deal with some tormenting personal problems. I was scared by what she was doing, but I could only be with her in whatever way I could and however she would let me. In fact, that was why I was slip-sliding along the River Drive toward our rendezvous.

In addition, my mother was dying, and my father was clinically depressed. My first marriage was unraveling, which pained and disillusioned me and my family, hurt and angered my kids, and put my professional future at risk. It actually was the end of the world as I knew it, and I didn't feel at all fine.

I turned off the drive and went past shops and department stores splendidly decked out for Christmas, lights, decorations, bell-ringing Santas, shoppers weaving along everywhere. I figured some of them must have felt as disoriented as I did that night. I know that Christmas is a tough time for lots of people. That year, I was experiencing it first hand.

I drove through the heart of the shopping district into a section where homeless folk camped out over steam grates in the sidewalks in front of stores whose owners had closed early and pulled down security grates over the windows.

I turned onto Lombard Street where row houses, eateries, and small shops existed cheek by jowl. I was lucky to find a parking spot a couple of blocks from the place where I was to meet Karen.

I got out of the car and looked around, as if waking from a dream. Then it came to me, two lines from a poem I'd read years earlier. Why just those two lines came as clear as from the poet's pen, I don't really know. Nor did I recall any other lines or even the name of the poet. Only two lines:

"This world is wild as an old wives' tale
And strange the plain things are."

The lines came like a visitation. That night, the world did seem wild to me, and plain things had become strange. And the night was still young.

The sleet had stopped, and the rain was a cold drizzle against my face as I walked down Lombard toward Vince's Tavern at the corner of 19th Street. Somewhere in the block between 22nd and 21st, I came across a row house with the whole front window jammed with a manger scene. Judging from neighboring houses, at some point the residents of this one had enlarged the window to twice its original size — probably to accommodate this exhibition! It was something you'd be more apt to see in a department store window than in a row house on Lombard Street. The painted figures must have been three feet tall, and each was lit from inside with glowing light. It was truly impressive.

I smiled as I hurried past, silently saluting the piety of the family who gave up half their living room and all of their privacy to display the manger scene in such splendor. Nativity scenes in South Philadelphia row houses are not uncommon, and yet "strange the plain things are."

I rushed on to meet Karen. We ate and talked. But the meeting didn't ease any of my anxiety or her pain. When we left Vince's, the rain had stopped. We stood on the corner and said good-bye. There on the street, I hugged Karen for a long time, and she hugged me back. I told her I loved her and asked her to be careful and to stay in touch with me no matter what. She promised she would. Then she went off to meet a friend, and I walked slowly back to my car.

I was thinking so hard about my daughter that when I came upon the row house nativity again, I was momentarily caught off-guard. This time I stopped to look at it more closely. There it all was: the coterie of shepherds, the three wise men, a full complement of angels, a number of assorted animals. They were all gathered around Joseph and Mary, who were side by side, looking . . . actually just about where I was standing. That was strange.

I stepped closer and examined the scene more carefully. My first impression had been right: There was no manger, no infant Jesus in the window! In effect, the street was the manger, and I was standing in it. Out of the corner of my eye, I thought I glimpsed someone smiling and nodding in the shadows behind the shepherds, but when I looked again, no one was there. Had that Lombard Street family intended that the street be the manger?

Intended or not, the scene was strange. The fragment of the long-forgotten poem crossed my mind again:

*"This world is wild as an old wives' tale
And strange the plain things are."*

What made those words float out of the near chaos of my life to the surface of my mind just when they did? Why had I come across that row-house nativity scene on my way to and from meeting Karen that night? I can't tell you. What I can tell you is the nativity scene made that row house, all the neighboring houses, no longer so plain but very strange.

And even stranger became the old familiar story that row-house scene was telling. That night, that old story was being told differently. This time those silent, lighted figures were looking expectantly out on the street for the Christ child, out on the street where the beasts are motorized now, and the milk comes in cartons, and the lambs wool in worsted suits, and people like shepherds sleep on steam grates, and people like wise men dish out food in soup kitchens — or work in political movements or business coalitions or churches to change things so someday there might not be homeless people or hungry children or addicted parents.

I stood there with tears in my eyes. With a force that lumped in my throat, I realized that just where I was standing, the Christmas miracle happens. In the street, where human traffic goes endlessly by, where men and women and children live and limp and play and cry and laugh and love and fight and worry and curse and praise and pray and die, just there Christmas keeps coming silently, insistently, mysteriously.

I turned and walked back to my car, the mystery of it making me light-headed and light-hearted. I laughed to myself as I thought about a wild stable always being close at hand in this wild world, about the strange, saving birth taking place in unlikely places like Lombard Street where I was walking — taking place anywhere I would ever walk, any street anyone would ever walk.

I stood by the car and looked in awe back down the street, trying to grasp the revelation of the strange, saving birth taking place again and yet again in all the unlikely places lining our streets — at the tables where we spill coffee and our secrets; in the beds where the sheets get wrinkled and the dreams disturbing; in human exchanges in taverns or cafés where our hopes for each other and ourselves stumble over our limited power; in the offices where decisions and lives are made, unmade, and somehow re-made. It happens in the shops where we search for some item that will be just right but never quite find it; on the corners where we dodge each other in our frantic pace, yet sometimes quickly explore each other's eyes, longing to make human contact in the midst of the rat race. It happens on the steam grates where, once in a while, passers-by fish a coin from their pockets and drop it in the hand of one of those homeless brothers or sisters.

Ah, yes, "strange the plain things are." A Christ come to be close at hand in unlikely people like that row-house family, and my family floundering as it was just then, and countless other families on countless other streets. Jesus born again and again, in a thousand times a thousand miracles, a thousand times a thousand moments, and an occasional heart. God close at hand. Always.

"God does something everywhere, but doesn't do everything anywhere." A teacher I loved said that once, and I keep forgetting it — and remembering it. I drove home that night, thinking of my daughter, my sons, and all the pain and struggles we would go through on our particular versions of Lombard Street. In that moment I knew that nothing could keep me from standing by and with my kids. And I thought of other people I loved, and those I didn't love much or at all, and I knew I would do the best I could to stand by and with all the "street people" of life because I had the God-given chance, the small, precious gift of doing something somewhere.

And it also occurred to me that one of the "somethings" God does everywhere — and certainly at Christmas — is to bring to an end the world as we know it. That doesn't make me feel fine, but it does make me feel better. Much better. Because the rest of the "something" is that then a new world begins in a small explosion of light no darkness can overcome.

In
The
Shadows

Clumsy Beautiful

They're always yellin' at me in this place, especially on busy nights like that one. When it gets so busy as that, the owner of the inn is fit to be tied, and maybe he should be. I suppose he's scared that if somethin' ain't just right, it'll make some customer mad, and he'll lose a few denarii. So, the busier the place gets, the more he yells. He yells kind of quiet, you know, like a snake hissin'. But there ain't no mistakin' what it is.

"Deborah," he'll yell. (That's my name and the prettiest thing about me, I've been told more than once — like I ought to have an ugly name.) "Deborah, get the wine goblets . . . sweep the floor . . . wipe up that vomit . . . get some wood . . ." and so on and on and on. Actually, he yells other things at me, too, but I won't repeat 'em. I try to ignore 'em and just do my job.

I'll tell you one thing they call me, though: Clumsy! I suppose I am, too, since I'm always droppin' cups, or spillin' wine, or trippin' over a door sill, or catchin' my dress and tearin' it on somethin'. People laugh at me, 'specially the customers, and they say crude things to me. I don't understand why my body won't do what I want it to. It's a source of embarrassment.

I'm clumsy with words, too, if truth be told. When anyone asks me somethin', and I have to answer, my throat gets tight and my mouth dries up, and I just go blank. Even with the other servants, I don't say much, though you mustn't get the wrong idea, thinkin' I'm shy and innocent or somethin' like that. I can tell a bawdy story

1st Day of Advent

good as the next one and hold my own in an argument, believe me. It's just that pretty words seem as hard for me to get hold of as the doves I try to catch sometimes out back. I been told it don't matter much, my bein' clumsy, since I'm just a servant and a woman. But that's what I wanted to tell you about, sort of. I wish I could tell you about it so you'd understand. Maybe I'll understand better myself if I can find the words. So, I'll try.

Oh, wait . . . another thing. I'm plain. I mean real plain! I think you ought to know that, though I ain't sure why, 'cept I think it's important for you to know me if you're goin' to understand what I'm tryin' to tell you. And the way a person feels about herself helps other people know her, don't it? I didn't say that too clear, but I trust you get my meanin'. Bein' plain is, well, a particular burden for a woman, I suppose.

Oh, men pinch and pat and feel when they can. And they're always tryin' to get me to do things with them, sayin' things to me they don't mean. And sometimes I go with them just for the attention, even for a few minutes. To tell the truth, I like the feelin' of what we do together, if you catch my meanin'. But sad to say, men don't mean nothin' *permanent* when it comes to me. Fact is, though, I ain't too much worse off than most women in Bethlehem, even them who get taken for wife. A little worse, maybe. Less secure than wives, probably.

Anyway, truth of it is, bein' a servant girl in an inn in a town like this ain't too glamorous. You get treated sort like of a beast of burden, a bearer of water and wood and dishes and nothin' much else, and you get to thinkin' that 'bout yourself after while.

But to get to the point, that day — or that night I should say — I was feelin' 'specially like a beast of burden. I'd been workin' all day. The town was runnin' over with strangers comin' in for the census takin'. The inn was so crowded and so noisy, you couldn't

1st Day of Advent

hear yourself think, and I had a terrible headache. I must have
been up and down the stairs and out in the shed and back, I don't
know . . . seemed like a hundred, two hundred times at least. I was
trembly tired, in a fog almost. I'd fallen over people's feet a couple
times, and once I just burst out cryin' and snuck into the pantry
closet for a minute. It had been like that all week, really, and now
it was halfway through the night and everythin' was still goin'
strong.

"Deborah, you mangy goat, get some more wood."

To tell the truth, I was glad to go outside. Maybe I could rest
a minute, quiet-like. Goin' through the kitchen, I grabbed a crust
of bread and slapped Nathan's hand away when he tried to get
fresh. I pushed out into the night air and leaned for a second on
the wall. "Bearer of wood and water and wine . . . and whatever
else men want . . ."

Goin' across the yard, I munched the bread, gulpin' it down
like I was starvin'. Suddenly I tripped and fell in the mud. Right
in the mud on my hunkies. Dropped the crust right in the mud,
too, before I'd finished it. I just lay there and caught my breath
before I started cryin', more from tiredness than hurt. Then I sat
up and started laughin'; I don't know why. Maybe 'cause suddenly
it kinda came to me.

What came to me was how wonderful still it was. The moon
was hangin' up there so silver and soft-like, and the clouds over
its face were touchin' it, gentle as I imagine a lover doin'. And the
stars were like someone just lit them like candles; and the darkness
around them had begun to crumple into tiny flakes like some old
shawl, and the flakes was fallin' away, floatin' down . . . like black
snow fallin' quiet all around me. And the cold and the mud and
the light were all quiverin', like durin' your first kiss and you
wonder what happens next.

1st Day of Advent

Funny how I'd never felt quite like that before or noticed how sweet bread tastes on your tongue before it goes down to calm your growlin' belly. Sittin' there, I felt like I'd waked life up, like it had been sort of sleepin' there unnoticed before. At least by me.

Then I heard a baby cryin' somewhere. I've heard lots of babies cry before, but usually it's just annoyin', 'specially in the night when you're tryin' to sleep. But this time I giggled at the sound. And wondered about it. So I followed the cryin'. And there in the stable, where old Naphtali works, was this family, a mother with her arm around a baby, jigglin' it sort of, tryin' to get it to stop cryin'. And what musta been the father with his arm around the mother, tryin' to comfort her. And this baby, a boy, obviously just born, red and wet, but so full of life it was spillin' out over everythin' around, includin' me.

I don't know what it was happened then. Maybe it was just noticin' that a new-born baby is like . . . like a miracle. I mean, there is this little thing, and it's alive. All its parts are there. It's breathin' and movin' and makin' little sounds. How does that happen? I mean, how does that *happen?* I just stared at the mystery. I don't have the words to tell you. It was life, pure and simple. I mean it was life, pure enough all right, but not so simple. No baby is, and certainly not this one. This one was makin' me breathe in gulps, like I couldn't get enough of that life he was about.

I *can* tell you that right then, lookin' right into the heart of life, or whatever you call it — spunk or hope or love . . . right then, and ever since, I felt beautiful. And furious proud, too, to be a human being, to be a woman, to be part of what produces a miracle like that . . . or *receives* a miracle like that . . . even *is* sort of a miracle like that.

See, I am clumsy with words. But all the same, I just felt, well, strangely graceful, about me and life and even about the owner of

1st Day of Advent

the inn. Imagine bein' that close, that much a part of the heart of
. . . of God, I guess. Yes, God. I do wish I could tell you better.
Maybe you got your own words. I hope so. I hope you know how
mysterious God is and how beautiful God makes people, even when
they are plain like me and got mud on them. Or blood, like the
baby. I hope you got the words for that . . . or the quietness.

1st Day of Advent

The Ninth Woman

In some things you have no choice. You just have to do them whether you want to or not, regardless of whether you see much purpose in them. It isn't until afterward that you may wonder about them and about why things happened just that way to you.

Off in Rome, Caesar Augustus decided on a census, and we had to comply. So it began. It may have seemed a little thing to him, but to us, it was a major disruption. There was a lot of talk, resentment. But no one could do anything about it. Everybody had to go to the place of their ancestors to be counted. We went to Bethlehem, Amos and I and our children, because that's where his family was from. The thing I couldn't figure out was why we had to be counted. Some said it was for taxes. Since we had nothing, anyway, such a long hard trip seemed doubly ridiculous to us. But we had to go, so we went. And little Deborah was sick all the way; burning hot she was. It is hard enough taking care of a family at home. Traveling, it's impossible. But you do what you have to do.

As it turned out, the afternoon we finally got to a place where the Roman legionnaires were asking people the official questions and writing down the answers on long scrolls, I was the ninth woman. I don't know why I remember that. The soldier asking questions called out for another to write down, "Amos of Godara, the fourteenth man on this day, with four male children, three female, and his wife, the ninth woman." And all the while, they were joking among themselves, paying little attention to us, really.

2nd Day of Advent

It was hard and bare, a number like that—so simple and matter-of-fact and distant, somehow. I remember shivering, and I remember my feet hurting and Deborah being so hot . . . the ninth woman . . .

Afterward, when the man said that was all and we could go, there was no place we could stay. Those who could afford it stayed in the inn. Some had family in Bethlehem who could put them up. We less fortunate ones, well, we did the best we could. A man Amos met said some people were being allowed to stay out behind the inn in a cave where the animals were kept. So we went. It was out of the wind. I remember the wind that night, and I recall hoping Deborah wouldn't get even sicker. We found some water for her, and we shared a little bread. It was a bit crowded, with all the people and animals.

Then . . . over in a corner of the place, this woman started to groan and make sharp cries like a wounded animal. I knew immediately what it was. I felt sorry for her. It wasn't much of a place for giving birth. But I knew I'd have to help, too, and that was irritating. I was so tired. Wasn't Deborah's being sick *enough*? And the other kids crying and being so restless? But, you do what you have to do.

The woman's eyes were wide, frightened. The pain seemed to surprise her. It often does the first time. Her husband didn't know what to do, except to keep reassuring her. Birth's too much for most men to understand. For most women, too, I suppose, but you have to take care of things first, then figure it out later, if you can. Most men can't do without answers before they try anything.

It took a while. It wasn't an easy birth. It was good I was there to help. Knowing how it was, I could tell her about it, and that seemed to calm her. I told her to scream if she had to and bite her shawl — not her lip. And I reminded her that the pain was helping the baby get out.

When he finally came, I cleaned him with a bit of crumpled straw, as you do a new-born animal. The father gave me an old blanket he'd gotten somewhere. I wrapped the baby and gave him to his mother. She was exhausted. And so was I, but I was glad I could help.

There's nothing like seeing what happens between a mother and a baby in that first few minutes. I've been there lots of times, helping in my little village of Godara. But never in a stable. Yet, the strange thing is, I felt it that night, too, that powerful, special thing between a mother and a baby.

The woman looked up and asked me what my name was. I told her "Leah." And she said, "Leah, this is Jesus." I smiled. It was the first time anyone had called me by name since we left home. Not a number, a name. It felt . . . good. I touched her forehead, and Jesus' cheek, and held her hand for a while, until she slept.

Deborah was still hot when I went back to my family. I lay down with her and held her very close. The children were all awake, but quiet in the dark. Just their eyes moved. They'd seen. It was like they were struggling with a secret and didn't know how to ask or tell it. And I didn't know how to tell them, either.

Some nights, like that one, the wind whispers, and it seems somehow like more than the wind. And children are quiet at the end of the day. Little things happen, and somehow they don't seem so little. But, it isn't until afterward that you may wonder about them and about why they happened just that way to you.

"Leah, this is Jesus."

2nd Day of Advent

Eyelight

Working all my life in a stable, I've seen lots of creatures born: sheep, oxen, donkeys. Most births are easy and natural enough. Some you have to help along. But, either way, you never get used to them. It's awesome to watch the struggle, to see the young one all tired and worn out afterward, and the mother, too. You can't help smiling, watching the mother washing her baby with her tongue. And then the little one working so hard and finally standing, all wobbly, and walking around all curious-like, but staying close to its mother. No matter how many births you've seen, each one squeezes your heart, all right, and makes you think about things you usually don't think about, busy as you get doing your work and trying to keep your life together.

But there was one peculiar birth happened once, long ago, that I won't ever forget. There wasn't any room in the inn. I knew that, working there, but it wasn't any skin off my nose. The stable and the animals were my business. I kept out back and left the rest to the others except when they made me help. So when those families came along and asked me if they could spend the night in the stable, I said if it was all right with the innkeeper, it was all right with me, as long as they didn't get in the way of my work or bother none of the animals.

It was really crowded in the stable because of all the guests, their beasts adding to the ones we had. You never heard so much bawling and whimpering. All night I was mucking out the place the best I could, trying to find enough new hay, quieting down the more skittish animals.

So I'd almost forgotten about those people I'd said could stay there until a man came looking for me and said his wife was having a baby. He asked if I had anything to wrap the child in after it was born. Such an interruption was all I needed on a night like that one! I was about to tell the man to see to it himself as best he could, when a light from somewhere outside caught his face just so. I don't know exactly what that light was. The moon? Someone passing by with a torch? A shooting star maybe? All I know is that it was strange. Even now, I shiver to think of it. And the wind seemed to rise up just then, too, like a spooked colt wheeling and galloping off across the meadow.

Anyway, there was that man's face in the quick light, I don't know how long . . . a minute, a lifetime. But I don't ever remember seeing a man's face so sharp and clear before. The deep lines around his mouth. His jaw muscles rippling his beard like a breeze caressing a grain field. And the beads of sweat over that upper lip where there is that little crease. (Jake, who works in the kitchen and is a little mad, says that crease is the print of the finger God lays right there to seal your lip just before you're born, so you won't speak the secrets of where you've been or the worlds where you've come from before you entered this one.)

But the man's eyes! His eyes were what stopped me. They were so deep. So tired, so sad, somehow. Yet, they were so strong — like they looked right through you; like they had looked right through almost everything and knew awful, wonderful secrets. Eyes that had the same kind of light as a rising sun touching the hill tops, then creeping down to the valleys, and seeing it makes you shiver inside. I remember those eyes. I guess the way to say it is that there was love in them, and . . . love always gives you pause

3rd Day of Advent

. . . sort of takes your breath away. Does mine, anyhow!

The man said a woman from another family staying in the stable was helping his wife. They needed something to wrap the baby in, cold as the night was. So I got a blanket. It was worn, but clean, because I'd washed it good after my dog, who used to sleep on it, died. My dog and his dying crossed my mind as I handed the blanket to the man and followed him to the corner where him and his wife had hunkered down. Strange how the cycles go: death and life being linked, one leading to the other so definite, so natural, but so mysterious all the same.

Anyway, I saw the birth. It wasn't easy, like a lot of them are. I don't know who fought the hardest against it, the mother or the baby. In any case, it appeared that neither of them were too sure they wanted it to happen. But nature paid them no mind. At last there was one final groan, followed by a sharp cry, and then a calm that was like that deep quiet moment just before or just after a storm. Even the animals seemed to sense something extraordinary was happening. They were absolutely still. I remember feeling that this birth was different, too, though I couldn't have told you exactly how.

So the woman who was helping wrapped the baby up in my blanket and handed him to his mother. The father's hands were huge and rough, and right then he put one hand on his wife's shoulder and the other on the baby's head. He was a tender man, I saw, for all of his being so big. The mother smiled, and she and her husband looked at each other for a long time. I don't know what their eyes were saying, but it was something powerful and personal and . . . secret I guess. I had to look away. Some things are private between just two, and if you interfere, even without meaning to, you're where you don't belong. But those eyes, I remember.

When I looked away from them, I looked to the baby. Now,

here's the thing I can't explain. That child's eyes were just like that man's eyes, just like his father's eyes. I know it makes no sense to say it, but it's true all the same. That baby's eyes seemed so sad somehow, yet so strong, with that same rising-sun kind of light in them, burning like they looked through everything, too, and knew awful, wonderful secrets. There was the same kind of powerful love in those eyes, and I saw it, believe me. Don't ask me more about it. That strange light that night, I never could figure out where it came from . . . or where the light in those eyes came from . . . or what made the wind sound like it did, like more than the wind. Like the wings of night birds flying, but you can't see them — just hear them.

So I remember, and I wonder about more things than I can ever mention without being called mad. And maybe I am mad now. But you do your work, and take care of what you can, and keep your promises . . . and you wonder. Especially when, some nights, the light from somewhere outside your window makes mysterious shapes on the walls and ceiling, like it's trying to tell you something deep and true. You remember and you wonder about the light and the shadows and about all you dare to know and yet know not. You remember because you can't forget them — things like birth and death and . . . love. Especially love. But even as you remember, you don't understand much. And yet you do remember eyes and light and those shadows and the very silence of them which seems to say, "Glory to God and on earth peace . . . peace . . . peace . . . *peace!*"

3rd Day of Advent

Tangled in a Line

ometimes you have to draw lines, and sometimes you have to bend them or even ignore them. But most of the time, you have to walk them; walk a tight line. The trouble is knowing which to do, when. When is the voice of conscience more critical than the voice of the court? You don't always know. It's hard to keep your balance. It's easier to compromise conscience than to challenge power.

So when Herod calls, you go! It was early evening when he called, the time I'm speaking of now. It had been a long day. The temple in Jerusalem is always a busy place, and priests have responsibilities . . . a thousand responsibilities . . . that often keep me awake at night: the wall of the temple needs repair; oil for the lamps is running low; revenue from sacrificial animals is off; there are the ritual observances to be got through.

And always there are political pressures to contend with — Rome on one hand, the Zealots on the other. Do you submit to powers or resist? And if you resist, how much, how far? And always the pressure, the pressure. When does one find time to think about such questions, to reflect, to study? I tell you, it's hard to keep your balance.

The days are always long, and this particular day had been one of the longest. We were meeting in the courtyard, the chief priests and the scribes, talking about how Rome's tax rulings were affecting temple properties, when the message came that Herod wanted us.

I remember feeling uneasy, as I usually do when summoned by powerful people. Rulers are not to be taken lightly. The nation must be preserved. Herod often wants the help, the blessing, of the priests for some scheme he's plotting. He is a cunning man. He could shut the temple down! He could get Rome to tighten the screws on our country. People would rebel, but . . . against Rome? It seems too terrible to contemplate. People would be slaughtered. This way, we give a little, modify, adjust, to keep the peace. But it's hard to know when to draw a line and when to walk it. Everyone knows that.

Herod summoned.

We went.

The palace was in a turmoil about something. You could feel it as soon as you walked through the gate. The guards were tense. There was a tightness in the air. The sun set fiery that evening, and the walls of the inner courtyard were blood-red up high, running down darker and darker into the deep shadows where we walked. I was seized with a sudden cramp in the gut. Perhaps I just needed to relieve myself. I felt clammy, but my mouth was dry as sand. Was it just pressure? Or something else? How do you know?

It was too late to turn back. Or was it? Perhaps my foreboding was for nothing.

In the outer chambers were three richly dressed men. They were obviously foreigners. They were just sitting there, nodding to us as we passed into Herod's inner chambers. There was a curious calm about those three men that added to my apprehensions.

When the door closed behind us, the air inside was heavy, rank. Fear makes the body stink, and Herod's breath was foul when he wheezed his question, his voice as tight as a tent rope in a storm: "Where is the Christ to be born?"

The question was totally unexpected. We were stunned. No

one thought to ask him why he wanted to know.

No, I thought to ask. Had the Messiah — the one we had waited for — had he come? What did those three men in the outer chambers have to do with this question? Had they brought news? What would Herod do if the Messiah *had* been born?

I did think to ask those questions, but Herod was obviously in no mood to be crossed. So I didn't! To challenge power is dangerous.

The torches burned in their brackets on the wall, and the occasional hiss and crackle of the flames made the sudden silence seem more ominous. The knuckles of the guards were white around their spears. It was quiet, as only fear can make it quiet. The air was so close you could hardly breathe. Another cramp hit me like a wave on rocks. Cold sweat broke on my forehead, ran down my back.

Every one of us priests knew what Scripture said about the Messiah's birth. So the answer Herod wanted was supplied:

> *"In Bethlehem of Judea: for so it is written by the prophet,*
> *'And you, O Bethlehem, in the land of Judah, are by no*
> *means* least *among the rulers of Judah, for from you shall*
> *come a ruler who is to shepherd my people Israel.' "**

Whose voice had filled the room in answer to Herod? Was it mine? Had I blurted out those words or had I simply thought them? In any case, the words echoed . . . a ruler . . . a ruler . . . a ruler. Herod was a clever man. What else should be said to soften those echoing words? Power is jealous. I said nothing else. We were . . . I was . . . just trying to keep my balance.

* *Matthew 2: 5b-6, NRSV*

4th Day of Advent

That's hard to do, isn't it . . . keeping your balance. Later, Herod ordered all the male babies in Bethlehem killed. All of them! To rid himself of the one Messiah. I can never forget that. Power is jealous, frightening. I can't forget that either. You have to walk a tight line . . . yet it gets tangled . . .

My responsibilities often keep me awake at night . . . and the memories . . . the massacre . . . and the cramps, the cramps . . . pressures, always pressures. Privilege on one hand . . . and I sometimes forget *what,* on the other. I wish God would make it clearer when you have to draw the line and where. If the Messiah survived the killing, would he make it clearer? Maybe Yes. Maybe No. Maybe both.

You know, what the prophet Micah really wrote was this:

> *"But you, O Bethlehem . . . who are one of the little clans of Judah, from you shall come forth for me one who is to rule in Israel . . . "*[*]

I wonder why, so long after Micah spoke it, we . . . I . . . tangled the prophet's line and why in the story of our meeting with Herod, it's recorded that way? "Bethlehem. . . by no means *least* among the rulers of Judah" rather than "Bethlehem . . . one of the *little* clans of Judah." There is a difference! One way suggests Bethlehem is much less than the other way — less and yet perhaps more.

In the night I hear a voice. Whose voice is it? Whose? It says, "Watch the lines . . . the choices . . . the little things."

O Bethlehem, so little, so little, but often a little makes all the difference.

*Micah 5:2, NRSV

4th Day of Advent

Under Their Noses

tudyin' the stars is a good thing, I suppose. Yes, I'm sure it is! When I have time, I look at 'em, and they are awesome, all right. I wonder what they are, and what keeps 'em up there, and what's behind 'em. But lookin' at 'em doesn't give me any answers to those questions, so I don't do it much. Yet, maybe just askin' the questions is a very important thing. For answers, I guess, you have to study the stars a long time. I don't know.

The three men who hired me as a tent bearer for their journey studied the stars like nothin' else mattered. They spent most of their time lookin' at the stars, talkin' about 'em, arguin' about old scrolls and maps like they held the secrets of life. And, as I said, I am sure that is a good thing, since their plottin' and plannin' got us to the place we were tryin' to get to.

But, I think, studyin' the stars can also lead you off the mark if you look at 'em too long. And if you look at *only* the stars, they put you in a kind of trance. You lose touch with other important things. You just don't see those things, you miss 'em. And that is not good — for the things missed or the ones who miss 'em.

The truth is, it was a hard trip over many days — or was it years? — from where we started to where we ended. A trip like that takes a lot of work. You have to pack food, measure it out, prepare it every day, and then repack it. You have to make fires, pitch and strike tents, feed the animals, rub 'em down, watch for pack sores . . . and a thousand other things. For such a long trip,

5th Day of Advent

three men like the ones I signed on with need a dozen people to help.

And that's what I'm tryin' to get at. They hired us and then ignored us. I don't think they meant to, but they did. They seemed to live in one world — the world of stars and supposin'. But we lived in another — the world of earth and people. When they needed us, they just took for granted we'd be there: cookin', cleanin' up, takin' care of what they must have thought was less important stuff. I bet it never dawned on 'em to tell us what they were thinkin' or what the stars were doin' or where we were headed. Like I say, I don't think they intended anythin' mean or bad. They were just too taken up with the stars, I guess. But to us, it came to the same thing as if they meant to ignore us.

Now, I admit feelin' a little angry about their bein' so blind to us, like we were not much different than dumb animals. I mean, we could have used some extra help once in a while, 'specially durin' some of the storms. But it was like they didn't see. That's the thing. They just didn't see what was under their noses. They were so totally caught up in what they cared about that they didn't see anythin' else. Now that I think of it, I realize the same thing happens to a lot of us, not just to people who study the stars. People get stuck in their own little world and shut out everythin' else.

What I'm sayin' is that, over that long journey, lots of things happened right under those stargazers' noses, but they just missed 'em, that's all. I mean, Abdul fell in love with Tamara, and it was like springtime with them, and us. And Elias, who stuttered and was so shy when we started, turned out to be a wonderful storyteller. Rhona played the lute for us so soft and beautiful you would 'a thought it was an angel makin' that music. And when Raman, who took care of the camels, got sick, Ardis mixed a bunch of herbs and mold and made a broth that broke his fever. When he started gettin' better, we all laughed and had a party with a bit of extra wine and scraps of meat and cheese that we filched from the stargazers who never even missed 'em.

There were lots of other things the stargazers missed, too. Like the way the ground shines when the early mornin' sun touches the dew; and the way a whole flock of swallows will fly this way and that, as if they were connected by some invisible thread, turnin' and dippin' by the same tug. I don't think those three men paid any mind to the way your breath puffs out in little clouds in the chilly air; or the smell of the jasmine; or the way rocks change their shapes when the sunlight and shadows hit them just so, as if they were livin' things. I swear, those stargazers never noticed a whole flock of things that made my heart beat faster or made me laugh, or that put a lump in my throat and made me whisper, "Thank you, God."

At last, we got where we'd been headin'. It was kind of a strange place. A stable. But the stargazers got out their gifts for the baby inside. I have to say they didn't seem like fittin' gifts for a baby — incense and spices and gold. Well, maybe the gold helped the family, but what I'm sayin' is that those gifts were picked before we'd even started, and those men were dead set on followin' their plans, no matter what.

Strange as it seems, I'm not sure those three men truly even *saw* the baby or, for that matter, the mother and father in that stable. I wasn't supposed to have followed them in. Not that they actually said not to, but that sort of thing is kind of an unspoken rule for us hired hands. But I followed anyway because I wanted to see what it was we'd come so far after. And it seemed to me that those three old wise men, if that's what to call 'em, didn't see that baby at all. I mean, they didn't smile, or touch his cheek, or kiss his head right there on the velvet-like spot on top, or any of that. It was as if, for them, that baby was really just as far off, as removed from the world, as the stars they'd been so busy plottin' about.

Funny thing . . . to have come all that way and still have missed it. At least, as far as I could tell, they missed it. I mean, we went back home another way just to throw off anyone who might have been wantin' to ask us what we were doin' there. But on the way back, nothin' changed between them and us. Nothin' else changed either. It's a sad thing when that happens. And it happens pretty often, as I see it.

It's not that those three were totally wrong, or anythin'. Or that lookin' at the stars is stupid. But, that baby . . . his eyes were so wide open. And it seemed the whole time I was there, he was lookin' so hard, strainin' to see, like he'd never rest 'til he'd seen everythin', linked up with all there was. It's like he was sayin' to me, to us all, "There are wonders all around you. Don't miss anything. Don't miss life . . . or God."

Way Over Our Heads

Naked Isn't the Last Straw

UNBORN: Why me?

ANGEL: I don't know. Why *not* you? Trust me, there's a reason. You'll find out.

UNBORN: Come on, do I have to do it? It sounds awful! What does it mean to get born, anyway?

ANGEL: Getting born is . . . well, it's entering a new place, a different place from where you are. And you have to become very small to get in. That's the way it's designed. There's no other way to do it. You have to start as a baby.

UNBORN: What's a baby?

ANGEL: A baby is a very small being. At first they're quite helpless. Oh, they have all the parts they'll have when they get bigger and stronger, only none of the parts work very well. Except certain ones. You'll see.

UNBORN: Helpless? *I know* I won't like that. I don't want to do it!

ANGEL: Someone will be there to take care of you. Probably.

UNBORN: Probably? *Probably* someone will?

ANGEL: Well, usually, your mother. And your father. Usually.

UNBORN: What are they?

ANGEL: Mothers and fathers? Well, they are . . . like other human beings. Only they aren't quite like each other. If they were, there wouldn't be babies.

UNBORN: It sounds worse all the time. I'm just not doing it. Why should I? I mean, what are human beings?

ANGEL: Well, I'm not sure what to tell you about them. They are creatures pretty much like all the other creatures God made. Only they are a little more . . . complicated, shall we say. They eat and sleep and walk around and have sex and babies. And they fight a lot over eating and sex, and who can walk or sleep where, and whose babies have what rights. But they think, too. Sometimes. And they love, once in a while, until it begins to scare them. They create things, and they destroy things. They struggle a lot. They are quite unpredictable, really. After all, they are free. And they keep looking for God . . . sort of.

UNBORN: Sort of?

ANGEL: Well, they can't seem to decide. They don't seem to know what they fear most: that they *won't* find God or that they *will*. So they "sort of" look, without concentrating much on how or where. But they don't seem quite able to *stop* looking either, especially when they are afraid, which is quite often. Only they don't like to admit it. So they pretend a lot.

UNBORN: That settles it. It's just too confusing! I'm not going to be born.

ANGEL: Excuse me? That settles it?

UNBORN: Oh, I don't know. Does it hurt, being born?

ANGEL: At first, while you're getting into the world.

UNBORN: Then it's over?

ANGEL: Not exactly. There are different kinds of hurt. That's partly what I mean about humans being complicated.

UNBORN: But why?

6th Day of Advent

ANGEL: Why what?

UNBORN: Why are humans so complicated?

ANGEL: I don't really know. Some say humans messed things up. They call it sin. And that's partly true.

UNBORN: Partly?

ANGEL: Yes, partly. Because I think humans are *meant* to be complicated, too. I think God created them that way. God put all those possibilities into them. That makes them complicated. I guess you'll be finding out why on your own.

UNBORN: I suppose so. But it sounds so depressing. I mean, what hope is there for such messed up creatures?

ANGEL: Hope? Oh, there's lots of hope. It's not depressing. You'll see.

UNBORN: I just *know* I won't like it. I'm going to apply for an exemption.

ANGEL: But you *will* like it! Really. Human beings are beautiful, too. And so is the earth.

UNBORN: Earth? What's the earth?

ANGEL: What's it like? Well, it's . . . a little like here. Sometimes. But sometimes not.

UNBORN: Well, that *certainly* clears things up.

ANGEL: What can I say? Earth is where human's live, or at least try to.

UNBORN: Fine. Just forget it. Just tell me where is this "earth" is.

ANGEL: Okay, come here . . . look . . . where I'm pointing. See . . . way, way over there, as far as you can see across all those thousands of light years . . . there, that little speck of blue. That's it. Can you make it out?

UNBORN: Barely. Makes me homesick just thinking about going there. I don't have to go yet, do I?

6th Day of Advent

ANGEL: I guess not. There is something else l have to tell you first.

UNBORN: I don't want to hear it.

ANGEL: But it's important.

UNBORN: Is it good or bad? I don't want to hear any more bad things!

ANGEL: I haven't told you anything bad. I told you some hard things about being a human being. But not bad.

UNBORN: Well, they sounded bad to me. All that stuff about human beings being complicated and fighting about things. And about there being a zillion kinds of hurt. Stuff like that sounds pretty bad.

ANGEL: Well, maybe a little. But not really. I told you, it's just because God gives human beings freedom to choose and puts so many possibilities in them and the world. Makes things interesting. Exciting. But not necessarily bad. And what I have to tell you now isn't good or bad either. It's just necessary.

UNBORN: Oh, sure. So, what is it?

ANGEL: It's that while you are waiting to be born, you start forgetting. By the time you're actually born, you'll have forgotten almost everything.

UNBORN: What are you talking about? Forgotten *what*?

ANGEL: You'll have forgotten everything we've talked about. You won't even remember me or having been here.

UNBORN: I won't remember anything? *Nothing*? What do you mean, that's not so bad. It's *terrible*!

ANGEL: But it really isn't. After all, if you did remember, you wouldn't really be entirely human. If you remembered, you might not take your life on earth seriously. You might think it didn't matter. And it matters. A lot. So you forget about "here."

6th Day of Advent

UNBORN: Forget *everything*? I'll never remember *anything*? In the slightest?

ANGEL: Well, you won't remember anything *exactly*. But sometimes, over the years of your life, you'll have certain feelings that you won't quite understand or certain longings or times of restlessness you'll wonder about. That will be sort of like remembering.

UNBORN: Doesn't sound much like remembering to me.

ANGEL: I didn't say it was exactly like remembering. It's just a *little* like it. And there might be other times when some kind of warm glow or . . . or shiver will pass through you, go over your soul, like a breeze over water, stirring up the very slightest ripple, and then be gone. But it will leave behind a trace of peacefulness or sadness or joy in you, or all three mixed up together. Those could be hints. Nothing specific. You won't remember anything specific about here or us.

UNBORN: Can I come back here? I mean, when I'm done being human, can I get born back here? *Please* tell me I can.

ANGEL: But you can't. Not really. Because things change. "Here" won't really be *here* then. Everything changes. You, me, everything. Being human will change you. Believe me, it will. That's what makes being human so exciting.

*UNBORN:*Everything you've told me about leaving here and getting born and never coming back doesn't sound exciting at all. It sounds terrible. Who ever wants to be born?

ANGEL: I wish I could make you understand, but I can't. I'll tell you a little secret. A poet wrote some wonderful words about it in a kind of prayer to God called a psalm. The poet said, "Thou hast made human beings little less than God . . . Thou hast given them dominion over the works of thy hands . . ." Sometimes I catch myself wishing I was . . . well, wishing that maybe I could see what being human would be like.

UNBORN: What are you saying? You don't mean that.

ANGEL: Yes, I do. At least sometimes I do. What I'm saying is that to be a human being is a wonder greater than the stars.

UNBORN: You really think so?

ANGEL: I really do.

UNBORN: That's hard to believe. Look, tell me plainly, will I always be a human being after I'm born? I mean, will I have to live on the earth forever?

ANGEL: So many questions! In some way, yes, you'll always be a human being after you are born. As for the other question, no, you will not live on the earth forever.

UNBORN: I ask for a plain answer and what do I get? Riddles and mysteries. Let me try again. If human beings don't stay on the earth forever, what *does* happen them? What will happen to ME? Just give me a simple answer.

ANGEL: Well, that's very hard to explain, but I'll try. What happens is . . . well, time passes, and . . .

UNBORN: Aren't there any simple answers? What's "time"?

ANGEL: Time is . . . well, look. See that galaxy over there? It's moving, isn't it?

UNBORN: Sure it's moving. Anyone can see that!

ANGEL: So, listen. For that galaxy to move from the place where you see it to the place it *will be* takes time. Time works like that with everything. Time measures movement and movement measures time. Get it?

UNBORN: No, I don't! And even if I did, what does that have to do with what happens to human beings?

ANGEL: Well, I'm telling you that time happens to human beings because they move, too. They move from one place to anther. Like galaxies, they move from where they were to where they're going. They move from birth through days and nights, through all kinds of experiences and struggles. Time measures their movement. That movement is their life. They get older as they move. After a while, they move to the end of their time, each one of them. Some have more time to move than others. But, finally, everyone comes to the end of their time. And then they die. Their bodies stop working. They have no more days and nights then. Now do you get it?

UNBORN: Die? I don't think I like this. It's hard to die, isn't it?

ANGEL: Yes, it seems to be. Human beings are usually quite afraid of dying. They wonder about it. They struggle over it long before their time actually ends. When it comes to dying, they are a little like you are about being born. They worry a lot about what will happen to them.

7th Day of Advent

UNBORN: Well, what *does* happen to them? That's what I asked you before!

ANGEL: I can't tell you.

UNBORN: You can't tell me. So what else is new? What *can* you tell me?

ANGEL: Well, I can tell you that human beings are not accidents. God planned them.

UNBORN: I must say you are *very* helpful. You scare me, you confuse me, you make it all sound so hard, thank you very much. What kind of a universe have we got here? What is God up to? Why did God have to make it this way?

ANGEL: Now you're way over my head. I don't know why. But I have thought about it, and I don't think God *had* to make it this way. God just *did* make it this way.

UNBORN: With a little help from human beings, if I'm getting it at all right. All that freedom God gave them, all those possibilities God threw in the mix.

ANGEL: Hey, you were paying attention!

UNBORN: But why this way? With all that freedom and chances for things to get messed up?

ANGEL: I told you, I don't know. But the same thing that makes it possible for things to get messed up makes it possible for things to get fixed up, made better. I think it has something to do with love. In some ways love seems to be the hardest lesson of all for human beings.

UNBORN: But why is love such a hard lesson for them? Love's the best thing there is!

ANGEL: I don't know. Maybe someday they'll learn. That's why God sent Jesus to be born on earth.

UNBORN: Why didn't they listen to him?

7th Day of Advent

ANGEL: Well, I suppose if they really had listened, they would
            have had to change, and I guess they didn't want to.
            Sometimes I ache for the earth. It's so small and
            fragile. Look at it over there.

UNBORN: It's pretty small, all right. But, I have to admit, it does
            look kind of beautiful, at least from here. And quiet.
            Is it really quiet there?

ANGEL: Not much. Quiet is another thing that human beings
            have trouble with.

UNBORN: Do they know about listening? They must know about
            that!

ANGEL: Some of them. A little. But whether it's quiet or not,
            they aren't sure what to listen for. Funny how they
            miss things, even when they hear them.

UNBORN: That's sad. Will I forget to listen, too, when I get born?

ANGEL: Mostly. But sometimes, maybe, you'll *almost* remember.

UNBORN: Almost? Not "almost." I *have* to remember how to
            listen!

ANGEL: Oh, there will be times when you listen and hear
            things, and you'll recognize them as beautiful, pow-
            erful, true things. Then you can practice listening
            more, and deeper, because you'll know how important
            it is. It's part of what humans call prayer.

UNBORN: But how will I know what things are beautiful and
            powerful and true?

ANGEL: Many ways. You'll learn. From some people, from
            your experiences, from your own heart.

UNBORN: Tell me one more thing. Something that's beautiful
            and powerful. Maybe I'll remember it. Just one thing.

ANGEL: Well, there are lots of things I could tell you. But one
            is that, sometimes, when it's a little quiet, mothers and

fathers listen to their baby's heartbeat before the baby is born.

UNBORN: They can do that?

ANGEL: Oh, yes!

UNBORN: What does it sound like?

ANGEL: It sounds like the heart of God.

ANGEL: Well, that about covers it. I've told you all you need to know about being human, for now. I think you're about ready to go.

UNBORN: Ready to go? Are you kidding? I still have a million questions! Besides, I haven't even packed.

ANGEL: Packed? You won't need to pack. You can't take anything with you.

UNBORN: Nothing? Not a thing?

ANGEL: Nothing.

UNBORN: But I have to have something to wear. I can't get born looking like this!

ANGEL: Believe me, you don't need to take a thing. You'll get what you need when you arrive.

UNBORN: But l have to make an entrance, don't I? I have to have something to arrive in.

ANGEL: No, you don't.

UNBORN: Let me get this straight. You are actually telling me that I don't get to take a stitch with me?

ANGEL: Not a stitch.

UNBORN: *You mean to say that to get born on earth, you not only have to forget everything you ever learned here, AND become small and helpless, AND risk being taken care of by human beings who are complicated and confused . . . AND survive with people who aren't too sure how to love or even know what love is, AND fight a lot about things, AND are afraid most of the time, AND get old and die and worry about it . . . BUT, to top it all off, you have to start out being absolutely, positively, completely stark naked? HAS ANYONE SPOKEN TO GOD ABOUT THIS? NAKED IS THE LAST STRAW!*

8th Day of Advent

ANGEL: Really? Why?

UNBORN: WHY? Tell me, are there people around when you get born?

ANGEL: Of course! Your mother is there, your father usually, several others.

UNBORN: Well?

ANGEL: Well, what?

UNBORN: Well, so much for going naked, is what! What'll they think when I whoosh in wearing my basic nothing? It'll be embarrassing is what it will be!

ANGEL: Oh, I see the problem.

UNBORN: You bet your sweet feathers you'd better see it. If human beings are so uptight about everything, I can just guess how they'll be about my turning up naked.

ANGEL: Not to worry. When you're a baby, nakedness is fine. In fact, they think it's adorable. It's only later that it's a problem.

UNBORN: Later? Please, try to explain that. Oh, don't bother. I already know: "It's complicated."

ANGEL: It is complicated, and it's even a little funny. You see, when you're a baby, nakedness is fine because . . . well, because to them, a baby's body is beautiful.

UNBORN: I begin to get the picture. It's later on that human bodies turn ugly, right?

ANGEL: No, that isn't exactly it.

UNBORN: For once, could you tell me exactly what it IS?

ANGEL: Exactly? Probably not. I suppose the simplest way is to say that it has something to do with the way people learn to think of themselves.

UNBORN: That's not even *close* to exactly.

8th Day of Advent

ANGEL: Well, listen. When humans grow bigger, almost none
           of them ever thinks his or her body is what they wish
           it was. It isn't beautiful enough, or strong or hand-
           some or thin or tall, or whatever, enough. They think
           their nose is too big or their ears stick out, or their
           eyes are the wrong color or their chin is weak, or
           their chest is too flat or their ankles are too thick,
           and so on and on and on.

UNBORN: Is it really that bad? Their bodies?

ANGEL: No. Not really.

UNBORN: So why do they think that?

ANGEL: They learn it. And then, to make it worse, there are
           things about how God made their bodies work that
           embarrass them, so they're forever making jokes or
           getting all puckered up about it.

UNBORN: That's closer to exactly but not close enough. Get
           closer. What are you really saying here?

ANGEL: I'm saying it isn't just their bodies that are involved
           when they talk that way. They're actually talking
           about how they feel about themselves and about things
           that frighten them — like being laughed at, or being
           humiliated, or not being liked, or being thought stu-
           pid. Or about sex. Or how it is to get old and die. As
           if those things mean there's something wrong with
           them or they aren't worth much.

UNBORN: But why . . . I mean, if God made human beings that
           way, why are they afraid like that? When they see a
           baby, why don't they remember?

ANGEL: Well, now, weren't you just saying things like that
           yourself? About why you didn't want to get born or be
           a human being.

8th Day of Advent

UNBORN: I suppose. But the more you explain it, the harder it seems to be a human.

ANGEL: Well, part of the problem is that human beings make it harder than it needs to be. They seem to have trouble accepting themselves as God's creatures, believing that God loves them. They seem to think it's bad to be a creature. They hide themselves. Behind clothes, pretenses, all sorts of things.

UNBORN: It sounds lonely.

ANGEL: Yes. It is. Humans get in a lot of messes trying *not* to be lonely. But they'll always be lonely because they are free. And they just become more lonely if they do things to try to make themselves less lonely. Do you understand?

UNBORN: Some. Not much.

ANGEL: Listen: Lonely goes with being human because God creates each human being as a particular person not quite like any other. It's a lonely thing, but a glorious thing, too. Loneliness is like a wind ripple on the water that God blows. It's like a reminder to turn to God and not try to stop the loneliness in other ways. Feeling lonely is a way humans have of remembering where they came from.

UNBORN: I'm not sure I get it, but maybe, sort of . . . I think I'm already beginning to forget. Does that mean I'm ready to go? I can't be ready yet! I have so many questions.

ANGEL: You always will. It's all right. Life is a mystery, a wonderful, holy mystery. You won't ever have all the answers, but you'll have enough. Listen to your heart. Pray. Look at Jesus. Don't be afraid. Listen to your loneliness. It's like nakedness. It hints at what it means to stand before God as a creature God loves. You can't hide or pretend with God. Loneliness is a gift to remind you of that. And that God loves you as a parent loves a child, naked and all.

UNBORN: I'll try to remember that. Will you come and visit me on earth?

ANGEL: Oh, yes. There are always many of us around. All the time.

UNBORN: That makes me feel a little better about going. I love you.

ANGEL: I love you, too. Try to remember love is what matters to God.

UNBORN: I know. But I'm already beginning to forget. How will I know when you visit? Hurry! Tell me.

ANGEL: You won't know, directly. God isn't obvious, so neither are we messengers. God keeps sending messages and messengers, but humans don't seem to pay much attention. Sometimes, some do. Maybe you will be one who does. But I *will* visit you.

UNBORN: Promise?

ANGEL: I promise.

UNBORN: Oh, I can feel it's time for my journey. That little speck of blue seems so far away.

ANGEL: But it isn't. It'll be Christmas time when you're born.

UNBORN: Christmas?

ANGEL: Jesus' birthday. Don't be afraid. Don't be afraid.

UNBORN: I'll try. Good-bye . . . good-bye . . .

ANGEL: Christmas is about peace. And joy. You'll find out. I pray you will. And it's not good-bye. God is with you. So it's always hello.

We
Can
Tell
You
A
Secret

The Thwig Eater

Care for a thistle, anyone? These purple ones are my favorites. You're welcome to have one, really. They taste a little like what you two-legged ones call "basil." No? Well, all right. I find them a particular treat now that I am a very old jackass, so you won't mind if I have another, will you? That's why my name is Thwig, which is what we jackasses call this purple thistle. Thwig loves thwigs. Hee haw!

I'm a dumb animal, really, but what everyone doesn't seem to realize is that all of us are really dumb animals, whether we have two legs or four legs or many legs or no legs. We are more alike than it might seem. Of course, you two-legged ones know many things we four-legged ones don't. But we know some things you don't, believe it or not. Which is why, just this once, I've been given the gift of speech to tell you what I can about the event, since I was there. I wish it were more, but I wonder if anyone could really tell more.

Anyway, I know the woman called Mary was very heavy as I carried her along that day. I belonged to her neighbor, Elihu, and she and her husband, Joseph, had borrowed me for the trip. It was not something I wanted to be doing, carrying this woman with a belly swollen with an about-to-be-born baby and then having to go so far from home with almost complete strangers. For me, it was a hard job, like hauling wool and wood and grain and jars full of water. Mary was uncomfortable and withdrawn. Joseph was withdrawn, too, and edgy. It seemed clear that they'd been fighting before we started. You know how you sense that sort of thing. Anyway, it was pretty obvious that they didn't want to be taking this trip.

Every so often he would growl, "I just don't understand," and it wasn't clear what exactly he was referring to — the trip, or Mary's mood, or some problem of his own, or what. And when she'd answer, "Well, I don't understand either," nothing got any clearer except that they weren't getting along too well right then. I tell you that so you'll know that everything about this event wasn't all "thwigs and clover."

The roads were clogged with people, and at certain places along the way there were Roman centurions urging everyone to move along faster. Occasionally there was a centurion riding some big, well-groomed horse who would prance around and go out of his way to bump me to prove how much better he was than I. He didn't have to do that; I already felt inferior. All my life I'd been called a stupid jackass, and I'd heard two-legged ones call others a jackass when they wanted to insult them. I knew I wasn't much.

I'm not sure I'm telling this very well. If all this seems to be about trivial, unimportant details, you'll just have to bear with me because that's part of what I have to tell you.

As we moved along that day, Joseph kept tugging more urgently on the rope until the bit began to cut into my mouth. He kept muttering to himself things like, "Damn Caesar, damn Rome, damn being too old for all this nonsense, damn Mary getting pregnant." He wouldn't stop for anything. And the faster we went, the greater the distance grew between him and the woman on my back.

And the longer we went, the more she complained about being uncomfortable, and about her worries over what were they going to do with this baby and how Joseph was going to earn enough to support them.

9th Day of Advent

Meanwhile, all I could think about was how much further did we have to go, and would there be anything good to eat when we got there, and would there be a place to sleep out of the wind. What I am telling you is that all three of us got to be little more than beasts of burden.

So part of what I have to tell you is that we missed things because we seemed to feel we were victims, that we had no choice but to do what we were doing. Nonsense! Even I have choices. Jackasses wouldn't be called stubborn otherwise! And if we four-legged ones have choices, how much more do you two-legged ones have them. Oh, not about everything, but about many things. We all have choices.

But choices are not just between alternatives. The secret of choices is deciding what those alternatives *mean*, what their consequences are, which choices are better than others and *why*.

Yet, for a time that day we were simply beasts of burden; and the burdens we were beasts of were our resentments. I'm not sure how it happens, but when you clop along obsessed with a routine, it's easy to start feeling sorry for yourself. At least, it's easy for me. The stones were biting sharply at my hooves, my mouth hurt, my back ached, and I resented having to do this job. I began to resent my owner for loaning me out. I thought about the thwigs I wanted and couldn't have. I thought about horses who weren't shaggy like me, who were more beautiful and talented, who had more to eat and better stables. Resentments grew like poisonous mushrooms in my dark mood.

Certainly you will understand if I tell you I think the same thing was going on with Mary and Joseph. I tell you this so you might see that everyone connected with this birth was something of a dumb animal. It is important to see that because that's exactly what made this whole thing so miraculous.

9th Day of Advent

As I said, you miss things when you clop along with your head down and your nose to the ground. *But the things you miss are still happening!* That's part of what is so amazing. Mary's baby still kicked around inside her, in spite of her worries and complaints. In spite of his grumbling and fuming, Joseph led us on. And I carried this miracle on my back, even though I resented it.

But one thing we four-legged ones remember to do that you two-legged ones forget is to keep in tune with all of our senses. As the day burned down, I heard a whir and looked up. The sky was the color of a thwig, and far off on the edge of the earth, two bright stars shone clear as a jenny's eyes when she sees her colt. The whir was the sound of children running at their before-sleep-games, though it sounded more like great wings in the air. Then the children laughed, and I swear you could smell their delight. And in the long shadows, I saw a young couple holding each other so tenderly I hee-hawed in gladness. Then, for the first time, I felt Mary's fingers tightly wrapped through my mane. Suddenly I realized she'd been hanging on like that for the whole time, and the courage and toughness of her hold stirred my heart. I'd almost missed it. Such a small, beautiful signal, my heart went out to her. I wonder how many creatures are hanging on like she was.

9th Day of Advent

o, we clopped along toward wherever we were going. But what I started to tell you is that you miss things when you clop along, counting whatever you count when you get into a routine, or become obsessed with a job or a list or a goal. You miss the dumb animal things, the little things, the precious things if you hold your nose to the ground. But, you know, you also miss things if you hold your nose up too high, if you pretend that you're *not* a little bit of a dumb animal.

I mean, one time I met a lovely mare named Chigachig. She told me that was her name because that's the sound she made when she galloped. Chigachig belonged to a wealthy man to whom Elihu sold wood. I met her when we took a load of wood to that house. Chigachig laughed at me for doing such lowly work and for looking so mangy. She said *she* looked like Ugo Oga (which is the name of the Great Mare who created all horses) because her coat was so shiny and golden and beautiful. I asked her if she'd ever seen Ugo Oga. She said she hadn't, but she was sure she looked like the Great Mare.

Well, since I had never seen Ugo Oga either, I couldn't swear that Chigachig didn't look like that god. But I do know that Chigachig missed many things about herself and the world because her nose was so high in the air. For one thing, she missed that I loved her and wanted to be her friend. And she refused to try the thwig I offered her because it looked dirty. Too bad for her.

But there is another reason I tell you about missing things if you hold your nose too high, a reason that is harder to get ahold of. When you start thinking of things too far off the ground, too airy, too sort of heavenly, it is easy to get your tail all twisted around.

I've heard the two-legged ones talking about their gods just

10th Day of Advent

the same way we four-legged ones think about Ugo Oga. The Romans say their gods are powerful and favor Romans over other people. But sometimes I also hear Elihu and his friends say that when God's Messiah comes, he will destroy the Romans and their empire and rule the world, and that Elihu and his friends and the people of their country will share his reign. That sounds as arrogant to me as what the Romans say.

Such arrogance makes you two-legged ones miss things just like we four-legged ones do. We are more alike than it seems, we dumb animals, and we all miss things.

I tell you this because in the twilight, that day, I heard Mary whisper to Joseph, "You said we are to call the baby 'Jesus'?"

And he answered, "Yes. According to my dream, he will be the Messiah."

And Mary answered quietly, "I know."

I wondered, then, about such a dream, and if it could possibly be true that a Messiah could be born to such dumb animals as these two (forgive me for putting it that way). And, if so, what might they miss about him? What were they already missing about him? What might all of us miss about such a Messiah?

It was a strange night. As we approached the edge of the village, the shadows felt heavy as water and seemed to part like the sea when the tiny ship of us moved through them. The dark leaves of the trees were streaked with strands of silver that scattered again whenever breezes rustled, then disappeared again to wherever breezes go. The smell of supper smoke and apprehension mixed together, and the quietness was weighted with expectancy. It was a lonely time for the three of us. Something was happening. We'd all begun to sense it, and our silence changed from sullen to thoughtful.

Finally, Joseph found us a place in a stable, which was

actually a cave with a rough opening on one wall through which the light and wind sniffed. It was a dirty, smelly place, full of other animals and some other poor people huddled out of the wind. The animals were caked with mud and dung. But it was shelter, and we entered it none too soon. Mary groaned, a sound as deep and loud as wind before a storm. The birth began.

Birth is an animal thing, drenched in sweat, bellowing, moaning, panting. It is full of blood and wonder. This one was no different, and the other four-legged ones and I watched, quiet, not spooked by the sights and sounds of it. This was something we understood. Or more truly, it was something we understood that we *didn't* understand, though we had been through it many times.

There is always pain involved when new life comes. It is not just physical pain, hard as that is. It is also the pain of being vulnerable, of birthing another life that will be vulnerable as well — a life separated from the womb where it was safe, protected; a life pushed out on its own; a life which, having begun, you know will one day end. So with the happiness of the birth there is also an aching kind of melancholy in that knowledge.

But without pain, life does not happen. Without pain, no one claims life, or reclaims it. Do not ask me why. I just know it is so in my dumb animal way. Without pain and struggle, life doesn't come fully to anyone. Without struggle, life itself somehow would be as unreal as Ugo Oga, as a god who is only an idea off somewhere where no one or nothing can reach — nothing like pain or sweat or joy. Birth is an animal thing. It is a precious thing. It is an earthy thing. It is a very mysterious and holy thing, a thing of God.

I wish I could say more, but I am a dumb animal. I can tell you that birth in the stable was a thing of God. That night the wind sang a miracle. That night the light of stars left scorch marks like a brand on the world. A strange wisdom gazed out of that little, red, wrinkled one's eyes, that baby Jesus. And I tell you, with this jackass tongue, that somehow I knew then that God was with us: with all us jackasses; with all of us dumb animals of the earth; with all of us who clop along with our heads down or our noses up; with all the sullen, raging Josephs, all the frightened, complaining Marys of the world.

I tell you that far off One — whatever name you give it, Jupiter or Caesar or Ugo Oga or Yahweh or Allah, or whatever — came to us that night. I know it as a dumb animal knows. There it was, *there God was* — a little thing, an animal thing, vulnerable as I am, vulnerable as a mother's love is, vulnerable as any love is and must be. It was a miracle God chose to come like that.

We four-legged ones know we live by gifts: thwigs and a bucketful of grain sometimes; a clear pool to suck water from, someone to scratch our ears sometimes because they care; a jenny or another jackass to run with or stand next to when a storm comes and jagged fire splits the sky and your courage shrivels. They're all gifts to make your blood rush and sing a little. We know we live by gifts, and we are not so dumb as to refuse them.

That birth was a gift! I received it gladly.

Will you understand this braying tongue if I tell you what I came to know that night? That night I learned what power really is: It is the choosing to come close, to break through the fences that separate us, to share yourself whatever the cost, to be vulnerable. A simple, complicated choice. That's all . . . and that's everything. Honestly sharing yourself is being willing to let yourself be a jackass . . . or a child, or a friend, or a lover. That is what love does.

Love is the only power we dumb animals really have. And I believe it's most of the power God has. So it must be the only power that matters much. I looked at that baby that night and understood

10th Day of Advent

just how risky a power it is, sharing yourself. That is what God did: God came to be with us, like a jenny in a storm. God came to help us claim life, and that is no easier than carrying that heavy woman, Mary, such a long, hard way, or the pain and labor of many struggles. And yet, life is joyful, too, as joyful as a back rub in the heart, a thwig for the soul.

 In that light-haunted, wind-fluted stable, the gap between God and us got closed. In that wrinkled baby, God gave us the way to touch each other's hearts, to close the distance between each other, to share ourselves, even with our enemies.

Yet we all, especially you two-legged ones, keep missing the chance. I know, because it was my daughter who carried Jesus into Jerusalem to die some thirty years after I carried him into Bethlehem to be born.

But I tell you, I carry him still. I cannot understand the mystery of it, but I carry his life in me now. Yes, I am a dumb animal, but what is beyond me keeps me going — the splendid puzzlement I saw in the birth that night. I hope the story of that night will carry you on, too, if you choose. For the wonder is that the things we miss *do* keep happening. The child stirs once more, even in the disbelieving ones. God comes again, and the labor and the joy of it await. Oh, don't miss things . . . little things . . . precious things . . . dumb animal things. Such holy things . . . such wondrous, holy things.

Are you sure you wouldn't care for a thwig? I find the smallest ones are a particular treat now that I'm a very old jackass. They really are quite wondrous.

Tickled from Behind

ello? Hello! I can't believe I can really talk like this, in your language! Quickly, listen up! I only have this power to speak your language for a short time, to tell you my story. If you feel stupid listening to a goat, think of how I feel trying to tell you anything in this idiotic language you speak!

Now, one of the main things I want to tell you is that someone is always out to get you. You think I'm exaggerating? Let me give you a little refresher course in my family history. Where do you think the term "scapegoat" comes from? You got it. My family history. I won't go into all the gruesome examples because you know about scapegoats.

The thing is, they don't even have to be goats any more, can you believe it? As a matter of fact, these days not only does everyone seem to *have* a scapegoat, everyone seems to *be* someone's scapegoat. It's not just that scapegoats are someone to blame anymore. Oh, no! The field has expanded. Scapegoats are someone to use, to con into doing something for you and taking the fall if it doesn't work out. And there you have the bare bones of what I mean when I say someone's always out to get you.

So, I'm telling you, you've got to stay alert, keep a sharp eye out. If someone is out to get you, you have to dance around a little, be ready to duck and parry on a moment's notice. Goats, you may have noticed, jump around a lot. Well, everyone has their own way of doing that.

11th Day of Advent

But, hey, having made that point, I'll get to the main part of my story. It's about a very momentous birth I was in on. The birth happened at night, but earlier that day my mate, Quan, and I had left the herd and climbed as high on the mountain as we could go. It makes me feel free and daring to leave the herd and climb like that!

It was cold up on the mountain, but it was as if you could see to the end of the world and beyond. There was snow on the high mountains across the valley. The grass tasted intoxicating. The air was so clear and sweet that only the tiny ripples on the little stream distinguished the air from the pure, fresh water. It was as if there were no other animals in the world except Quan and me. I said to Quan, "Let's never go back. Let's live up here, free, on top of the world. No one would bother us here. No one would take your milk any more, or steal the kids to butcher or barter. No one would threaten us. No one could get us. We could live all to ourselves. We could do as we please. We'd be free, Quan."

Quan nuzzled my neck and said, softly, "No, Zub. We wouldn't be free; we'd be a lie, a dream. The mountains are beautiful, and I love it here. But there are other animals in the world, Zub. We could never live all to ourselves. Praca and Capra didn't make us that way. The gods go together, so their creatures go together."

She rested her chin on my back. I felt troubled.

Praca and Capra are the goat gods — Praca, the Billy god; Capra, the Nanny god. To be honest, I didn't have much truck with such nonsense, but Quan did. I knew I couldn't get anywhere arguing with her, but I tried anyway.

"Look, Quan," I said, "let me tell you the way it is. In this world, which is the only one we have or know anything about, you have to look out for yourself because no one else will."

11th Day of Advent

She shook her head. I knew she'd start in about our owner, Naphtali, looking out for us and our friends among the other goats, so I cut her off first.

"No matter what it looks like to you, animals are out to get each other, Quan. Believe me. You have to keep a sharp eye out."

She pulled away and looked at me. "Why?" she asked simply.

I confess I couldn't explain the reason. I was just mouthing off without really thinking. So I couldn't look back at her just then. The answer to her question seemed so obvious, somehow; and yet, just because she'd asked, I knew it wasn't. She seemed so beautiful and wise to me.

Finally, I just blurted out, "You just have to look out for yourself in order to *survive*. I don't want to die, Quan."

And there it was, out in the open — my fear. I am afraid to die. Death is something I worry about a lot. I wonder when it's coming, how it's coming. I leap across chasms in the mountains as if I were fearless, but it's a cover. My knees shake every time I jump!

Somehow it was a relief that now Quan knew about my fear, but her response surprised me. (I think she'd always known.) She walked over and stood beside me for a long time, and then she said, "I think what you mean is that you don't want to lose your life, Zub."

I was confused and wanted her to explain, but she was silent. I waited. For a long time we stood looking out over the valley, watching the shadows climb toward us until we were standing in the last sliver of light, a light that was so dazzling it seemed to come from nowhere. It was like a fire that burned only on that little outcropping of rock on which we stood. Then I heard the words, though I couldn't swear she spoke them: "It is your life you fear to lose, Zub, so you cannot stay here. If you do not make sacrifices

11th Day of Advent

for something, nothing is worth anything. Not even life. Especially not life."

Suddenly I felt dizzy. Was it the heights, the light, the words? Whatever it was, the world was spinning.

The next thing I remember, we were slowly picking our way down into the darkness. When I looked back to where we'd been, I saw that the splinter of light still burned, intense and clear. But somehow it seemed to have leapt from the rock to a place higher up in the sky where it appeared to be a radiant star. The next thing I remember, we were slowly picking our way down into the darkness.

When we reached the valley, I wanted to stay out under the stars, but Quan needed to be milked, for she had come fresh, even though the kid she'd birthed had not lived. If we went to the stable, Naphtali might milk her, though he might be too busy working in the inn, especially since there were so many two-legged strangers about recently. In any case, we went to the stable, a cave out back of the inn. But we had scarcely entered and begun to get comfortable when all the confusion began.

A man and a woman pushed their way in, stumbling over us in their rush to find a place to lay down. A jackass followed them. Strangely, I wasn't immediately angry or suspicious — just surprised. I didn't resent this intrusion for some reason . . . maybe because obviously they had other things on their minds.

Anyway, it wasn't unusual for poor people to take refuge in a stable — or even for a woman to get pregnant in a stable, if you'll forgive my goatish candor. But it *was* very unusual for a very pregnant woman to enter a stable; and this one was obviously about to give birth. She groaned, then gasped at the pain. So the birth began. We watched.

Will you believe me if I tell you that watching the birth had the same effect on me as standing high in the mountains that afternoon, where it seemed I could see past the end of the world? I kept hearing Quan's words: "If you do not make sacrifices for something, nothing is worth anything. Not even life. Especially not life."

Then it was over, the birth itself, I mean. Things happened quickly after that. The man cut and tied the cord, and the woman took the baby boy to her breast, under her shawl. Quan went over and nudged the man, and somehow he understood. He found the milk bucket and milked Quan. Then he did a strange thing. He took the little baby and washed him off in some of Quan's milk. Quan watched as if the baby were hers. After that, the man took a cup and gave the woman a sip or two of Quan's milk and drank the rest himself.

He went and got a ragged piece of blanket somewhere, maybe from Naphtali, and wrapped up the baby. The woman kept whispering his name: "Jesus." I walked over and stood next to Quan and looked at the baby. I had the powerful sense that that baby *wanted* to be there. I mean right there, in that cold, dark, smelly place, which in that instant seemed somewhere past the end of the world and yet close to the beginning of another one. I think he wanted to be right there with us . . . us goats, so to speak. I remembered what Quan had said about gods and creatures going together, and the funny thing is that what she said felt different in this stable than it did up on the mountain. Here, it felt right.

That Billy-goat-of-a-kid even seemed a little like a goat, the way he was making snorting noises, kicking his legs so furiously, butting his head against his mother's breast. So I started to laugh and, to my surprise, Quan joined in. Then the jackass brayed, a bird sang, a dog howled, a cat meowed, and, I'll tell you, it sounded like music. The laughter joined with the wind and light that sniffed

11th Day of Advent

around the openings of the stable. Then it broke out and rolled out over the valley, getting louder as it washed down over the plains.

I laughed because the situation struck me funny! Here I was, always on the lookout because someone is always out to get you, and lo and behold, this tiny, wrinkled baby had gotten me that night, right in the heart, and it was wonderful. This baby, this dirt-poor, peasant mother and father stumbling into this forsaken, dung-drenched stable, had snuck up on me from behind and caught me off guard and tickled me with the whiskers of mystery . . . of God.

I swear, that little, unlikely thing, that newborn miracle, whispered to me of God and made my heart leap around like a billy-in-love. There was such a gladness in it all. Yet at the same time, there was a silence in it, inside me, that was wondrous as the stillness on a mountain summit in the moonlight.

I realized during that night that it cost this newborn one something to be there, in that dark, cold stable with us goats and jackasses and two-legged ones and all the others. It occurred to me it always costs a kid something to be here in this world. What was funny, joyously funny, was that, judging from his curious smile, this Jesus must have decided we were worth it, for him to make a sacrifice like that — to *be* with us.

I looked at that baby lying there, eyes wide open, gazing right at me. And I began to feel he was asking for some sort of sacrifice from me. And then it dawned on me: He just was asking me to be a goat and be glad of it. He was asking me to accept the sacrifices which being a goat involved. Nothing more, nothing less.

That night — that improbable, cold, smelly, altogether wondrous night — I went to that kid, that Jesus, and I knelt down by him. There was a fleck of blood on his cheek and a bubble on his lips like kids get, and that crazy smile. But in his eyes was a star,

I swear it — a dazzle of light like the one on the high mountain that shadowy late afternoon. What light was it? It was like no light I'd ever seen, and yet it was like every light I'd ever seen. It was like all the stars in all the skies that ever were, gathered in one place and then, in a blink, scattered wide again, forever.

As I gazed at that light, I heard him chuckle, a chuckle I'll never forget the sound of . . . baa . . . baa . . . Oh, I'm losing my speech; I must be quick to tell you now.

Oh God, my heart was full that night. So I did a funny thing, a spontaneous thing. I wanted to give the baby Jesus something, so I lay down and put my whiskers on his little feet to keep them warm. It must have tickled because his chuckle seemed louder, almost laughter. Quan's eyes twinkled as she lay down beside me and put her head on that tired father's lap to keep him warm. At last we slept a little. But every once in a while, I thought I heard the baby laugh, and it woke me. I know that, once, when I woke up, the little Jesus lurched forward and touched my head, here, between the horns; and to this day my heart burns from the power of it.

As I lay quietly, looking at the baby, I began thinking of Quan, and my goat friends, and even Naphtali. I began thinking that what's important is laughter and what it's made of . . . like delight and . . . well, gratitude, and hope, and love. What's important is this mysterious link between me and Quan, and between . . . well, as she said, there are other animals in the world and you really can't live all to yourself. What's important is a nuzzle against your neck and laughing for the joy of it.

Laughter is a holy thing. It is as sacred as music and silence and solemnity, maybe more sacred. Laughter is like a prayer, like a bridge over which creatures tiptoe to meet each other. Laughter is like mercy; it heals. When you can laugh at yourself, you are free.

11th Day of Advent

So . . . baa . . . quickly, quickly, before I can no longer speak your language . . . I want to tell you . . . baa . . . stay alert. Listen for the laughter. Listen deeply beneath all the words, beneath the silence. In the gurgle of a baby, in the bleating of a goat. Oh, join the laughter. Laugh at yourself, laugh in joy. Baahaa . . . for not to laugh may be to miss the one who is being born among us even now . . . and is out to get you . . . so keep a sharp eye out . . . listen . . . Watch . . . Laugh . . praise be, praise baahaha . . . ha ha . . . ha ha . . .

11th Day of Advent

Trillia Minor

ow that a mysterious power has enabled me to turn my
language of song into your language of words, I'll tell you
featherless ones a secret: Often I hear you sing, just as you hear
me. Your singing draws me to you, just as that night I flew into the
stable when I heard the baby crying — which is a way of singing,
too, you know. Oh, what a night it was. I will tell you of it, for that
must be why I have been given the gift of being able to speak in
your language.

That night, the flock of us flew on and on, as if there were no
time; as if the glorious twilight simply forgot how to become night
and lingered on, touching the edge of day like a lover unable to
leave his beloved. I cannot explain how the light shimmered all
around us, yet if you looked for its source, anywhere, all your eye
caught was darkness. Was it a strange tilt of the moon, or some
peculiar fall of starlight? Or, more wondrous still, was it perhaps
the darkness showing its other side? It's a mystery I cannot fathom.

All I can tell you is that there was a glow that night so awesome
that it stirred in us an irresistible urge to fling ourselves toward it,
though, in truth, it seemed to penetrate us as well, until we
glistened in the sky like drops of water flung into the twilight air
where they catch the last rays of sunlight. Maybe you have known
such nights.

Ah, that night was wrapped in wondrous sound as well. It was
like a thousand brooks tumbling over rocks in the mountains, like

a choir of nightingales scaling the vault of heaven, like the tinkling bells of the lead sheep of every flock on earth . . . all at once, everywhere. Yet, when you cocked your ear to catch it, there was only stillness and nothing moved. Was it the wind, or the rustle of our wings, or the beating of our hearts? Or, more wondrous still, was it perhaps the silence whispering its other side? That, too, is a mystery I cannot fathom.

All I can tell you is that the sound that night stirred an irresistible urge in us to lift our voices and hurl them to join that splendid spill of music. Oh, such a night of silver and song it was, a night such as you have surely known.

Soaring in that forever sky, I heard the baby's cry. Do you doubt it, that I could hear such a cry while flying so high? Oh, doubt it not! Yes, I heard the baby cry. I left the flock and flew to where it came from as if that were the only place in heaven or earth that it mattered for me to be. That is where my story begins.

I entered the stable silently, gliding to a rafter braced to hold the roof in place. Everything was old there, the stable as ancient as a cave in which Adam and Eve might have stayed, with the feel about it of a hundred generations of forgotten families who might have made their home there in times past. The animals were heavy with the aura of age — or agelessness — that animals easily acquire. The birth itself was as old as time, as were the primitive, fretful renderings of the parents.

Yet everything was new, too, as new as life, as new as something beginning and, so, triggering other beginnings, especially for the mother and father who were half-lost in their contemplations, occasionally looking at each other shyly, wanting to touch with words but managing only with fingers. I realized that everything about that night, everything about the silver and song of it, spun around this scene.

12th Day of Advent

Most of all, I watched the baby. I could scarcely believe it, but he watched back. I have never known one so freshly hatched who could watch so intently, for so long a time as this one did. Perhaps my quick movements had caught his attention. Whatever it was, he seemed never to take his eyes off me. He was all eyes! I swear it. He saw me! He was the only one who saw me that night in that place. Do you have any idea how amazing that is to someone like me? Do you know how cheaply birds are valued in this world, how we are taken for granted?

Yet, he was all ears, too. I know that because, when I sang, he heard me. But did I really sing? Or was the sound of it the other side of silence humming through me? No matter! He heard my song, the one in my heart; the one I wanted to sing and somehow must have.

So now you know the strange secret in the heart of my story: I thought I came to that place to see something, to see who had cried. But, no! Somehow I realized I came there, to that baby, to be *seen*! To be *heard*!

Oh, my featherless friends, I ask you, do you really think we go anywhere, any of us, just to search for something, just to see something that might be for us the key to understanding things, or to find something that will satisfy our ravenous hearts? Do you really think that is why any of us moves so fast, tries so hard, works so long? Oh, maybe the answer is partly 'yes.' Maybe we're always looking for something that will make the secrets of heaven and earth known to us.

But more than that, what we really want is to be seen. Not merely noticed, not put into a cage, a category, but to be truly *seen* — to be delivered into life by a gaze, gasping like a baby, startled into awareness by a look so penetrating, so powerful, that we sense forever after that we are known and will always be remembered.

12th Day of Advent

That's how it was that night for me, an ordinary swallow. He saw me, Trillia, the only Trillia that ever was or will be. And when he did, there was a rush of fire and wonder in me that, ever since, I've poured out in a song that I taught other birds to sing. To me, it was as though that was why he was born. It was to see me; and to see everyone else in that stable, every other creature on the earth, to see us so we would forever know we are seen.

Oh, I am such a bird-brain. I told you that baby was the only one who saw me that night. But that isn't right. Part of the secret of it is that *I saw me,* too! Maybe for the first time, I saw me that night . . . because he saw me. And so I sang that night, as for the first time.

I wish I could sing for you now. We birds sing just as naturally as you rejoice — no more, no less. For us, it's the very blueness of the sky, the warm shafts of sunlight, the abundance of bugs and seeds, and sweet dew in the morning that set us singing. These, and dry nests and a mate and little ones so fierce in their longing to fly.

But, like you featherless ones, we seem to lose most easily what is most natural. It isn't that we stop doing those natural things; it's that we lose *why* we do them, what they mean. We lose the *life* in them.

What I'm trying to tell you is that all of us creatures lose our natural capacity to wonder and to rejoice. We get tired, or stuck. Or jaded. Then we act as if we've seen it all. But it's just an act, and underneath we keep looking for something that will help us understand things, something that will satisfy our ravenous hearts. So we pretend not to look, yet look anyway out of the corner of our eyes so others won't notice. That's such a sad split in our lives. It makes us pluck the feathers off wonder and nest in envy.

I've noticed you featherless ones don't sing with your hearts in it much any more. You make the sounds, but there's no song if

12th Day of Advent

your heart's not in it; there are only notes, only techniques, only pretense.

There is a saying among us swallows which is, "You can't sing if you don't hear the song." I sing because that night I heard the song, and the song was simply, "You are seen. Always and everywhere and forever." My featherless friends, we are not lost. We do not live and leave no trace. Not a bird falls to the ground without God knowing. That's the song at the heart of everything!

I know, some of you are saying that swallows don't sing. Well, mostly you're right. Oh, sometimes we sing, some of us. But mostly we twitter. You know twitter, don't you? Twitter is our universal creaturely language. Twitter is what comes out when you sing and think that *you* are what the song is about.

Of course, you know twitter. You hear it everywhere, in every gathering you ever go to: the way people can't wait to talk about themselves and twitter away to impress you with what they know, or who they know, or what they've done. Twitter is what happens when you sing for your supper — you know, sing for gain, to get noticed, to get something from others for your singing. Then your heart's not in it, and the song is flat and empty.

But the thing to see is that under all our twitter is a deep longing — in us and in other creatures — to be *seen*, to be *loved*. That longing is why we all twitter. We want to be important to something, to someone. We want to prove that we matter, that somehow we won't be forgotten, that we are not of little value or no consequence. Oh, how much we all need to be seen! That's what I realized that night when he saw me.

Much later, when I slipped out of the stable and flew again, I simply could not contain the power, the incredible love of that baby's gaze. I rode that gaze as high as eyes can see, as high as you yourself must ride your dreams sometimes. I rode it to the stars.

12th Day of Advent

I flew with the angels that night, though I cannot tell you now of their appearance, what their raiment was or the number of their wings. Oh, do not doubt it. I flew with the angels that night.

Then, I looked down. What I saw is the rest of the secret in the heart of my story. I saw things differently. You can imagine that, can't you? You can imagine how, if you hopped from where you are to over here or over there, or if you flew higher or lower, you could look at the same things you'd seen before and see them differently. You can imagine how maybe you could even look at the past or the future and see it differently, too.

Well, I looked down that night on the earth, and it was lovely beyond even singing of it. I could only be silent, the other side of singing. Everything was laid out in beauty so wondrous and holy I closed my eyes and let it hold me. There I was, suspended somewhere between now and evermore, a tiny bit of a thing in an enormous creation. But what I felt was not so much how small I was, but how inseparably *connected* I was to it all, to everything, to the brightest stars in the heavens, to the dullest stones on earth.

That's what I want to tell you now, my featherless friends. You are a part of it, too, part of that enormous, splendid, mysterious whirl of life. A very small part, yes, but a part still, and inseparably connected. Oh, don't let yourselves become so earthbound, so timid and hesitant about those vast spaces, outside you and inside, that you forget, or disbelieve, that you are part of a holy thing, part of the song. So rejoice! That is the way to be part of it all and to grasp that God is with you in everything.

Oh, quickly now. Sing! For this is the most curious mystery of all: Incredible and glorious as the song is, it isn't the song but the *singing* that matters most! The mystery is that the song has many parts — parts for swallows, sparrows, and nightingales; for angels and four-legged creatures and those who swim in oceans,

12th Day of Advent

and for all kinds of featherless ones. The truth isn't that there is only one song for every creature; it's that all the different singing of all the different creatures mysteriously combines into one song.

It's the singing that matters, being a little part of the music. The music is God's gift in us, so the music becomes much less without each of us singing. Our part is to sing our music back to God with whatever ruffles and flourishes we can add of our own.

Oh, friends, be done with twittering. Sing from your heart. Dare to rejoice. For it takes courage to sing from the heart — courage and craziness. With a brain as big as yours, my featherless friends, it is a terrible temptation to think too much. To sing, you have to let yourself become a little crazy. Or a little child-like or a little bird-like. You have to let wonder have its way with you.

Dare to sing. Singing is the heart of the celebration of Christmastide, singing the birth of the One who is all eyes. His gaze is always there . . .

> God is there, looking back at you wherever you look;
> there in the eye of every crazy bird you see;
> there in every song you hear;
> squinting at you whenever the wind blows,
> wherever the light shines,
> whenever a baby cries or a child laughs,
> or a woman dances or a man sweats;
>
> God is there looking at you,
> claiming your compassion, demanding your response,
> wherever a family hungers
> or a creature is oppressed or brutalized
> by war or threat of war,
> by poverty or prejudice, by injustice;

12th Day of Advent

God is there looking at you
wherever beauty is done,
or truth is told, or lovers whisper.

Oh, friends, there is one unshakable reason to sing —
the baby born that night grew to be an adult,
and he insisted with his life
that God has an eye on you
and will never, never lose you in the dark.

God is there, looking back everywhere, in everything.
You are seen. See!
You are seen. Sing!

I tell you this because these are the few words I, Trillia Minor, will
ever speak. Now I only sing.

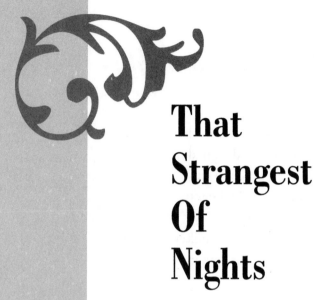

That
Strangest
Of
Nights

A Twist of Hospitality

sharp knock on the door, then urgent words
from one half-hidden in the shadows:
"Please! We need a place to stay.
My wife's birth pains have begun.
The time is here, we can't delay."
Through the night's din and flickering light
his voice came sharp as a hammered spike
to split the air, and
though then I knew it not,
my armored heart as well,
and the sum of time,
and my well-stitched, seeming seamless dream
of making a killing from Caesar's scheme.
Later, when the frantic became a vacancy,
I was grasped by a hospitality
far surpassing any of mine.

No, I did not turn them away.
We have a tradition in our land
to extend hospitality
any possible way we can
to strangers, especially those in need.
They needed a place, I provided one,

out of the wind, some privacy — a modicum,
a dry corner out back with the animals
and a few other travelers who huddled
in other corners of the stable for a penny or two.
Best I could do in those circumstances
They took my offer and paid their coins.
Then I left them there to take their chances.
It was I who blindly turned away from them.

Since, I've come to see
that all of us are travelers
from here, to somewhere, to eternity!
We travel not by Caesar's but by hope's decree
that we might come upon some small thing
that will make some larger sense of us,
of our mysterious beginning and our end:
a word, a silence, a fragment of song,
some signal at least fractionally clear,
as came that night, in a woman's shriek,
a baby's cry, the humming of the wind,
when the night breathed deep, gathered all in,
then moved to the dawn of what would be.
That is the story I would tell of me
and this twist of hospitality . . .

I'd been brutally busy for days with little respite.
Circumstance spawned a once-in-a-lifetime chance.
I felt compelled to seize it at all cost
as if it were drink to a parched throat.
My mind whirred in calculation every minute.
My heart beat fast at the prospect of affluence.

13th Day of Advent

Were the stars out? Was there a moon?
Was the night quiet as snow or full of whispers?
Was the wind a lullaby or a warning?
Did shadows dart in the streets like Zealot spies
scattered by the torches of Herod's soldiers?
Was there a melon-scented mist rolling in?
I cannot tell you.
I was busy with numbers, measuring portions,
setting prices, estimating profits.
Praise Caesar, I thought, what a killing I'd make!
But I did not send those two poor peasants away.
I kept the custom reluctantly.
It was myself I turned away.

When I'd shown them the stable, I checked my accounts
in a closet alone where I totaled amounts.
Yet my mind kept wandering from the trail of profit
to the maze of myself, my deceits that corrupt.
But, I'm a good man, I thought, I've earned what I've got.
I've worked hard, tried to keep every law I've been taught.
I'm not much for splitting philosophical hairs,
I keep my mind focused on practical cares.
Add things up, I maintain, the numbers don't lie.
Cut deals while you can, dismiss the nebulous why.
That was my creed, to make a killing my goal.
My intent was to stop short of selling my soul.

That night I had my list, bent on keeping close count.
I would trace each transaction and watch profits mount.
Yes, I considered my list as a sacred thing.
I studied like a priest so I'd live like a king.

Fifty mugs of wine in each of twelve flasks,
times two denarii each, while the wine lasts.
Eight squares of cheese, twenty bushels of flour,
twelve roasted lambs, fifty guests served each hour . . .
I subtracted a bit for the cheap lutist I hired,
and the cost of his food so his voice wouldn't tire . . .
(I'd been told spirits improve as songs entertain
and keep attention off food, so guests won't complain.)
I thought I'd been shrewd to arrange everything,
to make, as it were, such a marvelous killing.

Then alone, in the quiet, I found myself thinking —
A killing? Is that just a manner of speaking?
Or is it somehow tragic, something quite lethal?
What had I done to feel so achingly hollow?
As if touched by a ghost, I started to pace,
My heart was pounding, sweat rolled down my face.
Why did it seem so quiet in there?
Why was it so cold? Had some danger come near?
My flesh was crawling, my scalp bristled with fear.
I clutched at straws. Was it something I'd missed?

I shook as I checked again with my list,
but just then my heart squeezed up like a fist.
Like a corpse too soon buried I fled from that tomb;
my list trailed like a shroud, like the wake of my gloom.
I was shocked by the sudden wave of laughter and song,
yet, those sounds drowned my dread of whatever was wrong.
Though I was revived for a time by the revel of guests,
I knew something other was needed before I could rest.

13th Day of Advent

But I confess, I never went to the stable.
It didn't occur to me there was any reason.
I had to swallow my panic, get a hold of myself.
I had to follow my list, get the job done
It wouldn't do to leave the guests unattended.

When the last of them had gone to bed,
I cleaned the place. There were things to do
to divert my attention, to straighten my head,
to ignore my heart, to turn away once again.
I swept and scrubbed, picked up, directed the help,
put things away, repaired a chair that was broken.
Like I always said, your time is never your own!

But, that night I began wondering,
if it's not your own,
whose is it?
That's a night question . . .
Somewhere among the dirty dishes,
I asked myself,
if your time is not your own,
then *whose* is it?

Silence answered! It dizzied me so I had to sit and hold on.
As people slept, silence deepened 'til I was nearly undone.
Then I found myself wondering what they dreamed of.
Was it, like me, of beasts and shadowy things?
Of lovers, perhaps?
Of some resolution?
An easing of the torment? An ecstasy?

13th Day of Advent

Dreams and labor —
I think the two are linked somehow,
as day and night are sides of time.
But whose time?
At last, I stood and went to work while they dreamed on.
Yet, somehow I realized we all were waiting, in our way,
for some healing resolution,
for an ecstasy,
for some joy that is more than momentary.
It came to me we are all waiting for love,
and tears filled my eyes at that recognition.
We were waiting for time to be fulfilled —
whoever's time it is, ours or . . . mystery's.

13th Day of Advent

As I worked with my wife and family that night,
I joked about dreams.
In their sagging weariness, my family took me seriously.
My wife stared at me as if she was seeing someone else.
Her reply came as from the depths of reverie:
"Dreams are like the wind blowing where it will.
Tonight, out there, where you did not come,
the wind blew a miracle into life.
Now the child sleeps, and the mother, too,
dreaming of the child and the cost of his birth.
A dream of love is a challenge to be embodied in time.
A miracle depends on the will to choose."
Her words seemed a kind of invitation. But to what?

My daughter seemed to know.
She spoke over her shoulder, pointing with her head:
"While you were counting, we visited the stable.
In spite of the smell, we watched.
For a lifetime, it seemed,
we watched a dream become flesh.
Over the flanks of muddy beasts, we saw life come.
It was an unlikely place, full of humming and whispers.
Still, where else do unlikely things happen?
But, you did not dare. You only care for numbers."
I wanted to protest, to speak of my sweats and shakes,
but, no matter that, she was still right.
I had not dared, so I did not speak.

14th Day of Advent

But my son did.
I'd never heard him speak so,
or listened if he had.
He spoke like the writer of psalms.
"I went, too, drawn by light that seemed to follow me.
I peered through night and lolled with cats and quietness.
In peace I met strangers whose faces I knew not,
yet I knew their hearts were like mine,
and like the heart of that new born one,
and yet not quite. Not quite!
We knelt there and listened to his breathing speak.
And we heard, I swear, his heart's haunting beat."
My son expected me to scoff, but I could not.
His passion changed our equation.
He was father to me on that occasion.

Yet, I never went.
I listened to their words, but I never went.
Pride or confusion kept me away,
or a habit I would not break.
I forged reasons from excuses to persuade myself
but they did so only partially,
and sufficed merely to paralyze me . . . as always.
I said no more to my kin, only to myself,
thus winning the argument but losing my way.
I thought their spontaneity was an extravagance,
a betrayal of the guests.
Of course, others would argue, there are worse betrayals.
Say what they will, I had my duties, and my lists.
I argued, what difference makes one baby, more or less?
There are bills to pay.

14th Day of Advent

Still I wondered, what more is required of me . . .
and what more do I require?
Those two requirements seemed not a match to me.
Nor, I complained, is there time for both.
A hundred steps across the yard
from here to where they were.
I did watch the shadows there a time or two.
I even hushed those men who yelled in the yard.
They tried to explain their exuberance,
I decided they were drunk.
What else but too much wine
would make them leave their job tending flocks?
I stayed with mine.

Bone tired, I walked and counted.
Ten steps from meat rack to cupboard,
four more to the door.
I watched from there, for a time.
Ten steps to the cellar; left for the bread;
right for the wine.
Back up to the kitchen to stir the embers
tuck the bread in the oven to warm.
Eight steps to the rack to stack the wine,
twelve more to the dining hall.
I swept the tables and set them for morning.
Back to the kitchen to check what was left to be done.
I looked at the sky from the kitchen door
on which that desperate husband knocked,
ran my fingers over the panel . . .
Then turned to squint at the rim of the world
to check how much time before dawn.

14th Day of Advent

At last I sat and now it was tears rolled down my face.
What was I do to? It was my job to keep this place.
There's always so much to be done,
and whatever the time, it's never your own.

Or is it?
Someone has to get the mugs and plates and set the table.
That night, the crockery on the table planks
sounded like thunder, or the babble of kings
shouting their demands, expectations, claims.
Or, it occurred to me in my stupor of fatigue,
perhaps crockery knocking on table planks
sounds like that knock on the kitchen door,
or how I imagine the voices of prophets sounded,
when they spoke not only of claims but of choices.
Choices . . . perhaps that's the heart of it.

A hundred steps from this hall to the stable —
I never went.
But now I see it wasn't a hundred steps
only one — the first!
It was a choice.
When there's not time for everything,
time is an invitation to choose.
I never went.
But now I see choices are steps the feet take
following the steps the heart takes first.
Choices are the identity time gives you
when you make them with your life,
and with your love,
until forever fills your time.

14th Day of Advent

I never went.
A hundred steps,
or a thousand from here to there . . .
or only one —
just a heart beat or a lifetime never taken.

I never went.
But there was this strange twist of hospitality
which is the heart of my story, and of me,
the innkeeper kept.
Dreams came to me as I sat and watched the dawn
come silver soft through the door
on which the knock and words
and the mystery had come
the night before.

I watched . . . I heard . . .
A tongue I didn't know . . .
Movement in the shadows . . .
The singing of a bird . . .
A rustling.
A merciful hospitality came to me.
Then my heart understood:
worthiness is not asked of us,
just receptivity.
Or perhaps the kind of faithfulness
that is part humble curiosity.
And wonder enough . . .
and plain worn down simpleness.
I heard what ears cannot truly hear.
In the wind, I heard a cry and then a laugh,

14th Day of Advent

it was the language of the child
brooding over my chaos, creating a world.
I saw the chain of light traced across the sky
and I fell in love
with the old wrinkles and familiar voices
of me and friends and family,
guests and all,
given life again somehow.
Lifetime become mine, undeserving.
In one moment born, a promise made, and kept,
in the time of a life.

I never went.
One came,
and there was here,
then was now,
and that's the miracle even for me.
Not into the Inn where there was no room,
but into the shriveled womb of empty me
came the fullness of a time.
Christ is born!
Not too late, for me or you.
For we are guests.
And there's the ecstasy,
the twist of God's hospitality,
eternity mysteriously
extended to us
in time.

14th Day of Advent

When the Shavings Sing

The Loneliness of Joseph the Carpenter

(JOSEPH ENTERS IN DARKNESS, CARRYING A LAMP, WALKING LIKE AN OLD MAN. HE TAKES COVERING OFF OF TABLE, PUTS LAMP DOWN, AND RUNS HAND OVER SURFACE. HE PUTS ON APRON AND TAKES RAG FROM POCKET, BEGINS RUBBING TABLE. STOPS. LOOKS UP. BEGINS TO SPEAK.).

It is me, Joseph.
For a long time I have not spoken to you directly,
but surely you have not forgotten me.
But for me it is time to speak,
for time runs short for me.
I made this altar for you as my offering.
Bit by bit it took my life to build it, and much pain:
to find the wood, to cut the parts,
to fit the joints, to make it stable,
to plane it smooth, to carve this paneled scroll,
to rub in oil so it would last,
and light caress the grain.

Each time, with the oil, I rubbed in prayers.
Not words such as I speak now
while there's such time as you allow,
but prayers, still, of tears and curses,
of broken dreams and rumpled loneliness,

as you also surely know.
Now words too long not spoken I would speak to you
and with the oil rub them as well into the wood
and thus will know myself, and seal for you,
what I have made and who I am.
I dare this, though you know that I'm a quiet man,
a carpenter who speaks better with his hands,
quiet, save for what has churned within,
this clang of lonely years and lonely thoughts
which I need tell you now, as if you didn't know.
For my sake, then, I speak, to find some peace.

Every year at this star-scorched time
I've resolved to tell you, and almost begun,
then pulled back into my too-willing unreadiness,
waiting for a smoother season in my life,
with no rough edge, no gnarl, no slivers,
no cracked place to have to work around.
It never came. I knew it wouldn't.

Ready or not, the time has come for this to happen.
for time itself has become the sliver. So I begin
with these words familiar to every Jew:
"Hear, O Israel, the Lord our God, the Lord is one.
Blessed art Thou, O Lord our God, King of the universe,
Who forms light and creates darkness,
Who makes peace, who creates all things."
But peace, Lord, you did not make for me,
at least not in a straight way or entirely,
even though I was regular at the synagogue,
reciting the prayers by heart again and again,

15th Day of Advent

though without my heart being wholly in them
as it is in this prayer I utter now.

O Lord, King of the universe, hear me
for my heart is open before you on this altar.
I am alone. It is my voice alone I lift to you.
Mary's son — and who else's? — was half the ache
I carried through these years,
hoping to be delivered of
before the fullness of my time had come,
not that I didn't love Jesus all the while.
Yes, I loved him, yet, from a lonely place,
outside, some distance between us,
knowing he was not mine.

Mary tells me now I am not able to travel with them,
for Jesus moves fast and I have grown slow.
She is right. But no more right than before.
I always remained behind and watched them go.
There was always work for me to finish.
We were never rich enough for me to go.
Mary tells me I forget things and might get lost.
Well, I have always been lost, a little,
not sure what she and he were all about.
But I remember much, O Lord.

I remember how it was before his birth.
Mary was poor and young-maiden plain,
though to these already seasoned eyes,
which saw fine tables in rough planks,
she was quite beautiful indeed.

15th Day of Advent

I was not a young man, nor handsome, as you know.
But my being able to provide made my desperation
seem to her to be the essence of devotion.

So the arrangements were made, such as they were,
between her family and mine,
and the deal struck for a small dowry.
But Lord, I being more than ready,
took no note of the small print
on what was to come after.
Yet even had I been able,
even had I foreseen her too-soon pregnancy
and my more long, labored pain,
I would not have even then withdrawn,
for I was blindly happy
before I saw at all
what love required of me.
That was the wager you won, O Holy One.
But it was a hard thing you put on me.
I did not get what I expected.
Whoever does? Did you?

But before our marriage, or the birth,
oh I remember well, O Lord,
that season of giggles and silliness,
of a sky full of stars, a heart full of song,
how we danced and sighed the scent of lavender,
were folded in silence, wakened in laughter
and lived in each other's eyes.
Oh, I felt young and it was lovely.

15th Day of Advent

Lovely, lovely . . . before she said,
"I am going to have a child."
There was no laughter in her voice then, Lord,
only sober truth, and secrets.
Secrets she could not fully tell,
for she did not fully know,
this being her first one,
she being so young,
yet suddenly so far-off wise
as a pregnant woman can sometimes become.
So unflinching as she was, telling me her news,
all other sound was walled away,
all light snuffed out,
and I felt suddenly as old
as I'd felt young but hours before.

Then came this gorging bitterness,
this humiliating loneliness,
this deathly sense of nothingness.
I knew the child she carried was not mine.
Whose then? Whose then? Whose then?
I gagged on those words.
I thought to walk away,
leave her to her shame.
I thought to take her by the throat,
choke from her the name
then go and kill the man.
But none of that would change the shock
of being caught between my dream
and this betrayal.

15th Day of Advent

O Lord, it is hard to be a man
when your manhood seems at stake.
Mary said she was pregnant by the Holy Spirit.
What was I to think at such an outrageous claim?
She had audacity, I had to give her that.
But little credibility.
You have to forgive me, Lord,
my doubt that You were the one,
the Father of the child rooted in her womb.
However much she may have wished it so
to spare her innocence, to preserve our vow,
my part was simply to provide what was necessary.

But Lord, do you engage so often in such begetting
that doubt of it should not enter my mind
at Mary's seemingly far-fetched explanation?
To ask you to forgive me that
seems to be asking very little.
And yet, if it be true, what Mary claimed,
that her condition was your doing solely,
and the Messiah was growing in her womb,
then for me to forgive you this insult
to my virility, of which you warned me not,
is, indeed, asking very much.
Who is any man to forgive you?

Accept then this altar I here offer.
With it hear my ancient accusations out
and let me be at peace with you
before time ushers me to sleep.
For at Mary's announcement

15th Day of Advent

the betrayal was a deed done,
the insult, a blow delivered
like the swing of a hammer
to the groin.

O Lord, King of the universe,
who was I to believe, who was I to forgive?
All I knew was that her child was not mine.
It was between Mary and whoever,
Mary said it was you.
For me, it was whoever.
The "between she and whoever" did not include me.
I was on the outside, excluded.
Exiled in loneliness and work and duty.
It is hard to be a man, you know.
If Mary spoke truly, you are finding out.
Or did you know all along
how hard, and how much help
we humans need?

O Lord our God, King of the universe,
it was the darkness you create that I knew then.
I groped on. It was Mary I tried to forgive.
Then the dreams came,
like ghosts haunting me to wakefulness.
Voices telling me to fear not
to take Mary as my wife
but not expect to be her lover,
an aching loss of our earlier loveliness.
Was it your voice, or hers, or mine, spoke so,
To take her as my wife and despite the shame,

15th Day of Advent

despite the slow, unyielding pain,
to willingly embrace this loneliness?

I stayed with her. You counted on that,
though you could have made another plan had I faltered.
I was expendable. I sensed that.
Even so, I stayed.
I wondered if I was just too desperate to leave,
an old man for whom a something relationship
was better than a nothing wilderness.
I stayed.

Was I just too weak to stand up for myself,
letting her walk over me rather than bringing her down?
Yet would causing her fall put me on my feet again?
I stayed.
Was it my wounded pride that wouldn't let me leave,
pride like a broken leg on a valued chair
that I was driven to repair
so as to prove my potencies had not been removed;
by whimpering pride driven to keep up appearances?
Who cared? Not you, but I.
Yet only at first. Then pride tired.
I stayed.

Or was it that I loved Mary
and love betrayed is still love,
perhaps deeper for being less
than a wine-and-flowers fantasy.
Yes. Yes, I stayed, yet a bit reluctantly.

15th Day of Advent

I became useful. And Mary slept alone.
There was no warm comforter against my loneliness.
Still I was useful. O Lord, you knew I would be.
Carpenters are. That must have been the plan.

So when came the enrollment demand
and off to Bethlehem we went. I got us safely there,
but scarcely there and bedded in a barn,
when her waters broke and he was born,
landing like Noah after the flood.
Lord, what I remember of that night . . .
was the cold. It got inside me, and stayed,
clanking like rocks, like stones,
flaying my heart to pieces.

What I remember was Mary's eyes.
They never strayed from Jesus.
He was all she could see,
all that mattered to her in the least.
And that was it.
I was only useful.
I wrapped Mary and the babe in my cloak,
found old skins in corners to cover them,
heaped straw around Mary's feet
and with my body shielded them from the wind.

But I could not rejoice as Mary did.
He was not mine.
A father cannot know the bond that holds
between a mother and a newborn child.
Still, we have our own bond that forms,

15th Day of Advent

different but strong. I'd dreamed of it.
Instead, Lord, I felt twice removed,
once from Mary and whoever,
once from this child who was another's.
I was at the edge of all of it,
huddled in barren loneliness.
He was not mine, this Jesus.

Oh, there were songs that night,
eerie in the wind. I heard them dimly.
Splinters of words about peace on earth, and joy.
For me those things were as far away
as where the singing came from.
I was exiled in usefulness.

15th Day of Advent

O Lord, blessed art thou for the chores.
I was glad enough for them.
It gave me something to take my mind off
what ate at my heart, some small purpose
to sustain me through the days.

So when he was two, this little Jesus,
there came other dreams to torment me,
full of screams and blood and awful warnings.
Was the voice yours that spoke
of Herod's terrible massacre of children,
a holocaust of the innocents?
I was told to take Mary
and this son who wasn't mine,
and flee for their safety.
They were my responsibilities.
I mattered for my usefulness.

The trip to Egypt to escape Herod's madness
was all bundles of rations, and ropes
and careful routes, and repairs on the run,
places to stay, bits of work to pay for things,
my chores, my duties.

Then came the trip back to Nazareth,
the frayedness of things, the short cuts,
short supplies, the weariness.

16th Day of Advent

I got us back, Lord.
You must have known I would
or I would have had no dream to go.
And I was glad for the work of it.
But it changed nothing between us,
between Mary and Jesus, whoever and me.
The stones within me clattered all the way.
Mary simply loved her child more
than she loved anything.
Jesus was hers, not mine,
in the way that can't be changed,
the way of flesh and blood.

So, you know, the years went
the way of all flesh and blood.
I was useful, but Mary still slept alone.
We shared routines, respect, civility.
There was kindness and care, no animosity.
We even had other children together.
But Mary always slept alone.
She withheld not her body but herself,
which was untouchable,
and she chose not to share.
I worked and was quiet.
I helped raise Jesus the best I could.
He laughed and had his own secrets.
He spent time alone, grew strong and thoughtful.

And when he was twelve,
the year of his passage to manhood,
we made the pilgrimage to Jerusalem,

16th Day of Advent

the pilgrimage required of every young Jewish man.
Then he was missing.
We frantically searched.
Finally, in the temple we found him.
In tears Mary spoke more sharply to him
than I'd ever heard her speak:
"Why did you do this to us?
Your father and I have searched everywhere . . . "

It was the first time she had ever called me that.
My heart leapt.
Was she signaling a change?
I looked at her.
Her eyes were locked on him
as on the night he was born.
"Didn't you know I must be in my father's house?"
His words made her smile.
To me they were daggers opening again the wound
I'd tried to stitch with forgetfulness.
They both knew he was not mine.
The father he referred to was not me.
He was loyal to another.
I felt not jealousy
only a void, a vacancy
in which the stones inside clattered.

But, I was useful, Lord.
You must know how hard I worked.
I taught him carpentry, and he delighted me.
He learned fast, was good with his hands,
though his heart was not in it,

16th Day of Advent

as mine was not in the prayers
we uttered together in the synagogue on Shabbat.
For both of us it was a duty we did
for each other.

Maybe that's how it began to change.
Was that part of what you had in mind?
If so, it was not without its cost.
One day while he was helping me,
our little cart stuck in slippery mud.
I watched as Jesus collected stones
to put beneath the wheels,
small stones, gravel.
He gathered them in his apron,
then held them out to me.
He said, "These are like those you carry inside."
I was stunned that one so young
would see me half so accurately.
He had a carpenter's eye.

Then he scattered them under the wheels of our cart,
and the wheels took hold, the wagon moved.
As the wheels squealed against the stones,
he said, "Listen to the gravel sing.
Everything has its song. Listen."
As our cart waddled along on our delivery,
he said, "Gravel gives traction.
That's why it is beautiful.
It sings of the kingdom. All things do.
You have given me traction, too.
Your work, your duty done,

16th Day of Advent

each day a bit broken from your heart
from dreams turned cold.
Traction you have given me
as I will give you by my love, my brother."

It was like him to say such words
and leave me with the mystery of what he meant.
Brother? Me? I was almost his father.
Well, no, but provided like a father,
cared, taught, watched, wondered like one.
Brother? Then related, at least. At least family.
I smiled. I loved him, too, this almost-son,
and yet . . . he was not mine.
Still, there was traction. I was useful.
The stones that rolled around in me
had become useful in my duty,
my work . . . and I was glad.

To be useful is to be part of some purpose.
I didn't know what it was,
or where the traction of me led,
but that is what he'd said,
Mary's strange son,
and not quite mine except . . . in part
as in his saying I was part
of something he was part of, Lord.

Traction from the stones of pain and disappointment
the simple fidelity of every day.
"The gravel sings," he said. "Everything has its song."
What was mine, Lord? What was yours?

16th Day of Advent

Traction is good, but is it enough?
Without it, nothing moves.
But moves where?
That remained the mystery.
Moves where? With whom?

He is gone now, Lord.
As usual these days, they are off somewhere,
my wife, Mary, and Jesus, her son,
and those who follow him,
as Mary does, being now as bewildered
as the rest of them, as I am as well,
for this mystery is as deep
as the promises it keeps.
But Jesus is not quite the Messiah
Mary expected, either,
doing those strange things,
saying what he does.
His riling people up upsets her,
as it upsets the rooted powers
against which she would protect him as a mother,
yet cannot.
Still she loves him with all her heart
and bewildered, follows him wherever.

They tell me I'm too old and too forgetful
to go along. But not in my heart.
There I follow him.
From a distance, of course, as usual,
but not such a distance, which is unusual.
He called me, "Brother."

16th Day of Advent

What shall I call him?
I asked him that as I ask you.
Before he left this last time, I asked,
knowing we'd not see each other again,
time having traction and running out.
He said, "Listen to the song of things.
Listen when the shavings sing.
They will sing to you what you long to know."

O Lord, I love the wood I make things of.
I made this altar for you as my offering.
One night as I was using the plane on the last board for this,
fitting it, making a rough place smooth,
I listened to the shavings
as they peeled away and fell.
I listened . . . and the shavings sang.
The sound was very like that night when he was born.
Or so it seemed to this old man.
O Lord, tell me the shavings sang!
Tell me this is not the conjuring
of a mind worn down by time.
No! I swear!

"Shoosh, shoosh, shoosh," they sang.
"He is not yours . . . not yours . . . not yours," they sang.
"You are his . . . are his . . . are his," they sang.
"You are like us . . . like us . . . like us," they sang.
"Your altar is made from us . . . from us . . . from us," they sang.
"We are part of it as much . . . as much . . . as much," they sang,
 "as what you see and smell and taste,
 and touch . . . and touch . . . and touch," they sang.

16th Day of Advent

"You are his . . . are his . . . are his," they sang.
"Be at peace . . . at peace . . . at peace," they sang.

Lord, you need not tell me this is not conjuring.
I was there when the shavings sang.
I did not expect their song.
I expect less, by far.
I expect the worst, the knots and gnarls,
the cracks and splinters.

I did not expect the singing.
That first time when he was born,
or this time from the shavings.
I did not expect Mary's son
to be of the Holy Spirit.
I did not expect a Messiah.
I did not expect you.
Not for years did I expect good news.

I did not expect this joy.
It is a gift.
It does not come on cue.
It's a surprise.
Who deserves it? None.
Who is it for? All.
For the shavings of the earth.

"We are part of it as much, as much, as much,
as what you see and taste and touch and touch."
"Listen when the shavings sing," he said.
But I did not believe they would.

16th Day of Advent

When they did, I was overcome, struck dumb.
O Lord, blessed art Thou, blessed, blessed, blessed.
These shavings are your mercy, Lord, to me.
Yes, mercy, mercy, mercy to me.
I accept it, yes. With joy . . . joy.

Now I see that joy is not loud,
or not always loud, or only loud.
Why had I always thought that?
How much singing have I missed?
Too much, too much, too much.
Joy is not always loud, like angels' choirs,
but more like choirs of shavings,
the gurgles of a newborn.
It starts in stillness,
the overcoming that shushes speech,
and touches the soul.
Sometimes in such a stillness,
such a joy, such mercy, I see things whole,
quickly, deeply as in a lover's eyes,
as in a baby's birth and star-lit skies.
A stillness, a wholeness, mercy and joy,
a purpose wrought in a mystery abiding.

I am part of this mystery
as these shavings are part of this altar I made for you.
Bit by bit it took my life to build it.
It is my gift, my thanks, my praise to you
for my life, and for the joy,
while there is still time to offer it
to you, his father, and mine as well.

16th Day of Advent

"Brother," he called me.
Brother to him
and so to everything.
Joy. Quiet as a carpenter.
Quiet as a carpenter's almost son,
Quiet as this brother to everyone.
Quiet as this strange savior come
who is not ours but makes us his.
Joy. I have listened to the shavings sing.

16th Day of Advent

A Wide Berth

The Shame of Michael the Goatherd

*(MICHAEL ENTERS HERDING GOATS, CARRYING BAG OVER
SHOULDER, BUNDLE OF STICKS BY A ROPE. PROCEEDS TO
SET UP CAMP BY SETTING STONES IN CIRCLE TO SHIELD FIRE
FROM WIND. HE TALKS TO HIMSELF AND GOATS.)*

This place'll do.
There, that's enough stones to keep the wind out.
And this rock'll be dry for sitting. Fire will warm things up.
> *(TO GOATS) Hey-ho, settle down out there.*
> *Get to eating. Plenty of grass around.*
> *You can come closer when the wind kicks up.*
Now, then, what've I got here? *(FORAGES IN BAG)*

I gotta remember to tell 'em
what a strange night it was.
Don't worry. I'll remember.
It was the strangest night ever.
Tell 'em there was more than one got born that night.
I can never forget that.
How could I forget? The strangeness that night . . .
it changed everything. How could I forget?
The thing is, they never listen.
They don't pay me no mind when I tell 'em.

17th Day of Advent

It's because I walk like I do.
Feet pointed at each other. Like an idiot.
I look like an idiot. Like a pigeon.
I know. It's the only way I can walk. But they laugh.
Makes me ashamed. How I walk. How I look.
I hate my body. I wish it was different.
I wish I was different. More pleasing.
I know I'm ugly.
And I'm always ashamed.
I always got something to hide.
Me, is what . . . myself.
How I am. Hide it.
I'm missing something. I'm maimed.
It helps to be a goatherd.
Nobody talks to you.

Maybe they're right about me.
I walk like a pigeon.
And I really ain't much smarter'n a pigeon.
Not when you come right down to it.
Yeah, first you can't walk right,
then you can't learn quick-like.
Even playing as a kid I got ashamed
at how slow I was catching on to things.
I'm stupid. That's the nut of it.
All you can do then is be a goatherd.
>   *(TO GOATS)   Hey-ho, easy out there.*
>   *Don't take no offense. No insult meant.*
>   *There're thing's worse*
>   *than being a goatherd, you know.*
>   *Though I can't think of one right now.*

17th Day of Advent

Time for some cheese and bread. *(FORAGES IN BAG, RETRIEVES)*
Women never come near me. None of them.
Don't blame 'em, really.
Every morning the first thing is the stink.
Last thing at night is the stink.
Wake and sleep with the stink.
You don't have to tell 'em. They know.
It sinks in, the stink does.
To my clothes. These are all I got.
When I can, I wash 'em.
Don't help much. The stink stays.

Gets in your skin, your hair, your mouth.
I can taste it all the time.
Stink comes from the goats,
the dung, rotten carcasses, sickness, vomit, old sweat . . .
But not to lie, I have to say,
it comes from inside as well,
that awful stench, that hellish smell.
Stink ain't just from outside.
It's inside just as much.

When I come near, they yell,
"It's Michael. Give 'im a wide berth."
Even the shepherds yell that.
They make jokes about me and laugh.
They think they're so much better than goatherds.
I guess everyone else thinks so, too.
Not to lie, I guess I do, too . . .
Give 'em a wide berth.
Give myself a wide berth. Ahh . . .

17th Day of Advent

At first I thought "berth" meant having a baby
and I got flustered and angry about that,
thinking the shepherds meant I was weak and womanly,
so I spit and dared 'em to fight me
if that's what they thought.
I didn't know what a wide berth meant.
I was ashamed I didn't know that,
didn't know much of anything.
I was stupid. Stupid!
But I finally learned it meant to avoid me.
To not come near me.
As if they'd catch my stink.
I wondered how they knew.

I gotta remember to tell 'em
what a strange night it was.
I remember, but they never listen.
It's a wide berth they give me.
Only Mosa and Pildash know
the strangeness of that night.
How do Mosa and Pildash know? They're goats.
And they weren't even there then.
They weren't even alive, so how'd they know?
How'd they know?
I told 'em, that's how.

> *(TO GOATS) Ho-hey, Mosa. You know, don't you?*
> *How strange it was that night?*
> *Pildash, you know.*
> *Samson, you know.*
> *I told you. You're good goats.*

17th Day of Advent

I talk to you goats because you're here.
There's no one else to talk to.
Except yourself. You talk to yourself.
Goats and yourself.
Maybe a stray traveler once in a while.
But mostly goats and yourself.
You get close to the goats.
They're not mine. Someone hires me to herd them.
For however little they want to pay.
Can't be choosy. So you take it.
Seeing who you are, that you stink anyway.
Yet you start thinking, acting
as if the goats are yours,
are owed to you.

I watched how the shepherds did it.
From time to time you kill one or two goats,
eat the meat, sell the hides.
Sell 'em for wineskins, bags, sandals,
make yourself gloves, a coat,
have a few shekels for a little wine.
You tell the owners a wolf got those goats, or a lion.
Now and then you bring
a ripped, bloody hide back to show 'em
so they won't get too suspicious.

Those are the tricks.
You cheat. You steal.
That's the nut of it.
You cheat, lie, steal for personal gain.
It's a way to try to scrub away

17th Day of Advent

the terrible stink, the ugly stain.
It's not a good thing at all.
It doesn't work. The stink stays anyway.
It just made me more ashamed.

And on a cold night . . .
On a cold night, the goats slept with me,
Sheva, Pildash, Mushi . . .
We huddled together. For the warmth.
Like lovers we huddled. Together.
It's an unspeakable thing,
being together like that,
goats and . . . goatherds . . .
this stinking goatherd
. . . like lovers.
According to the religious law,
you could be . . . stoned to death . . .
if anyone even accused you . . .
goatherds have been stoned.
> *(TO GOATS) Hey-ho, you don't have to fret.*
> *No, Sheva, No Pildash . . . you don't fret.*
> *It's the advantage you have as goats.*
> *No shame for you . . .*

Me, it shamed, the stink. That I stink.
I was ashamed of the way I walk,
the way I look, what I do,
how slow I think, how bad I stink.
The way I am, even now a shame . . .
a great shame.

17th Day of Advent

That's why I must remember . . . remember
to tell 'em what a strange night it was,
of the strangeness that changed everything.
I remember but they pay me no mind when I tell them,
even as the wind sings,
even as the fire crackles,
even as the stars glisten
and gather like goats to listen,
they pay me no mind when I tell 'em.

So you talk to yourself . . . to myself,
and to the goats, one more time . . .
and one more time
and one more time after that,
one more time like this.

There are times when the goatherd stink
is in your throat,
an ache is in your shoulders and knees,
and in your heart,
and you're sure God himself
has given you a wide berth.

Not to lie, I'm not religious in the usual sense.
For that I can't get near enough
to where the chanting and the praying is.
I can only get to the courtyard of the animals,
where they're bought and sold and sacrificed,
the bulls, the lambs, the doves, the goats,
where my tears at losing these friends
flows down the drain with their blood.
No, I'm not religious in the usual sense.

But you can't live under the stars,
or hear the singing of a bird,
or watch anything, even a goat, be born,
or see death stalk a creature
like a lion in the grass,
or see a mother goat fight the lion
for her off-spring,
or watch a lily open
to trumpet a welcome to the sun,
and not be religious at all,
not wonder if your ache will ever ease,

18th Day of Advent

or if you'll ever be
welcomed home somewhere.

From your mother's breast
it seeps into your Jewish bones
to expect a Messiah
to come someday —
never today, of course,
but someday, just the same —
come like a king to make things right —
not for me, a goatherd, of course —
for the righteous, not the shamed.
A Messiah someday, but never today.

Nevertheless, when the rumor came it was exciting.
It snapped the snarled string of day after day
after day after day after day . . .
The rumor was passed to me from a old woman.
From time to time she visited herds to buy milk.
A bony, scraggly-haired, toothless hag she was.
I liked her.
She was a woman. She spoke to me.
I never wanted to see her leave.

Keturah was her name.
She made cheese from the milk
because it was soft for her to chew with her gums.
She gleaned tufts of goat hair, sheep wool
from where it snagged on bushes
and wove them into ragged clothes.
Some said she was a witch

or possessed by demons.
That, I'd never say.
She talked to me. She spent time with me.
It didn't matter how she looked,
no uglier than me anyway.
I thought she was strange, all right,
but maybe more angel-strange
than demon-strange.

Who says all angels have to be
clean and beautiful?
They might be terrible and frightening,
some of them, breaking in like that
from some eerie, other world.
That is, if you believe in them,
which I do . . . a little more now.
> *(TO GOATS) Hey-ho, I see it.*
> *Don't get in an uproar.*
> *It's just a little lightning. That's all.*
> *Won't hurt nothing. Calm down.*
> *Just a little lightning. It'll be all right.*

Anyway, that day, a little before that strange night,
Keturah walked over,
came from the shepherd camp
a hill or two that way
where she'd spent a few days.
She told me there was a crazy woman
living with them shepherds.
Keturah said the woman seemed to be getting
crazier every day.

18th Day of Advent

Turned out the crazy woman had been there for a while,
living like a prostitute with them, Keturah said,
being a prostitute in return for food
and a little protection.
We both laughed about the protection part,
us knowing the shepherds
(and me knowing myself).
They treated the crazy woman bad, Keturah said.
Used her hard, treated her mean.
Said from what she'd seen
the crazy woman might be with child.

Keturah said she thought the shepherds
were becoming afraid of the crazy woman,
her getting more crazy all the while,
that, being done with her,
they would tie her hands and feet
and leave her for the wild animals.
Keturah considered going back
to be with the woman,
watch over her some.
It was a tasty tidbit of gossip, Keturah's story,
something you could keep company with,
play with for many long nights.

But it couldn't hold a candle to the rumor.
Keturah said everywhere she'd visited lately
there was talk of the Messiah coming soon.
People said they'd seen mysterious lights in the sky,
heard strange noises,
felt rumblings in the earth.

18th Day of Advent

Keturah asked had I seen any signs?
Felt anything?
Did I notice anything strange?
Of course, you see things, hear things, I told her,
but no more lately than usual.

Except maybe for the wind humming a sound
a pitch higher than before,
and perhaps the stars seeming to droop
a little closer to the ground,
and the goats being more wary and jumpy
about sounds they usually ignore,
and, like a while ago, more sheets of lightning
without any storm coming after.
There was nothing more I could remember,
nothing more, though since she'd asked,
even that little seemed strange.
No, it didn't seem strange; it *was* strange.
I remember it.
Of course, I remember. It was strange.

Keturah nodded as I told her.
Then she told me to stay watchful.
She was sure the Messiah was on his way.
I scoffed, but I stayed watchful.
Even after Keturah left late that night,
I stayed watchful.

18th Day of Advent

If I hadn't been watching,
I wouldn't have heard the noise.
In the moonless darkness two nights later,
or maybe it was three, I heard the noise.
It woke me up. I listened carefully.
It wasn't the goats. They were strangely quiet.
I laid still, frightened.
The air seemed charged as it is before a storm
but the stars were out and it was cloudless.
I got up and squinted into the night.
Dark forms flitted down the hill.

It was the shepherds running, wild, fast, like a game,
like it was day time, not pitch dark,
like they could see where they were going
and wouldn't trip and break a leg, or worse,
on the unfamiliar ground.
And they were shouting as they ran,
"Come on. Run. Run to Bethlehem
before it's too late. Come on, run, run."

It was two leagues or more to Bethlehem,
an hour's walk, or two or more
Yet you could tell they were going to run all the way.
The voices faded and it got quiet again.

I checked the goats.
It was as if they'd heard nothing.

19th Day of Advent

It was all very strange.
Then I heard more footsteps in the darkness.
Someone else was running, slow,
panting like a wounded animal.

I called out, "Stop! Who are you?"
Whoever it was stopped. Nothing moved.
I waited. Then I circled slowly around
like you stalk an animal.
I followed the panting,
and came on that still shadow from behind.

It was a woman. She was young but grimy, worn out.
The rags she wore were wet and sticky
and those on her feet were almost in shreds
though her thin shawl seemed a lovely, eerie white.
Strange that I noticed that so clearly.
Sweat poured down her face. She seemed in pain.
I knew it was Keturah's crazy woman, the prostitute.
She was round-faced, round every way,
round in what she said.

Before I could ask her, she pointed,
then screamed in a mixture of pain and excitement,
"Bethlehem. Messiah.
Have to go before it's too late . . ."
She turned away, gasping.

"Where's Keturah?" I shouted.
I felt like I was in a roaring windstorm.

19th Day of Advent

The crazy woman screamed back,
"She will meet me . . . on the way back."
She groaned and doubled over.

"The Messiah? How do you know?" I shouted.
"Visitors . . . in sky . . ." she screamed,
"Go . . . see."
And she took off running.

She kept screaming until you couldn't hear her anymore.
It's hard to tell if a scream
carries joy or pain or fear or need,
or all of that and more.
She was gone before you could make sense of it.
But I remember.
How could I forget
the strangeness of that night?
So I tell 'em yet one time more.

> *(TO GOATS)* *Tell you, Pildash, Mosa, Samson.*
> *No one else will pay me any mind except myself.*
> *You love this story that you've heard before.*
> *It'll help you sleep.*

Though what I tell of did not in the least
help me to sleep after the crazy woman left.
The darkness seemed spent. Thin, drained.
I couldn't sleep.
Finally I got up and followed them.
To Bethlehem.
Slower even than the crazy woman
with my pigeon walk.

19th Day of Advent

But I went.
The darkness was very thin when I got close,
and a curious silver haze as from afar
seemed to be leaking through it
here and there like the quick tail
of a summer's falling star.
I pondered, What had made me bold enough to come?
Why was I not too ashamed?

Then, emerging at the edge of town
I could make out the shepherds,
coming in my direction,
moving stealthily as shadows,
going back fast as they came,
to reach their undefended flocks
before some disaster struck.
I did not see the crazy woman with them.
Where was she?
Where was Keturah now?

The wind was blowing wild again, and biting cold.
As the shepherds came near,
I yelled to ask them how to get there,
where the Messiah was.
Soon as they knew it was me,
they gave me a wide berth.
They never pay me no mind.
There was nothing to do
but go off in the direction they'd come from,
looking for rich peoples' houses,
a palace maybe,

19th Day of Advent

fitting for a Messiah's birth.
But nothing stirred anywhere.
No one appeared.
I wandered aimless-like, confused.

At last, remembering the goats,
I began thinking I should turn back.
But first I wanted to find
a shelter out of the wind,
to rest a spell before setting out again.
in that cold, howling gale.
Perhaps I have the nose for it,
but that's how I found the cave
behind an inn, where animals were kept:
I smelled my way to the place.
To keep from being seen as a thief,
I snuck in quickly, quietly
and, in spite of the stink,
peered around for a corner
where I could lie out of the wind,
and suddenly . . .

I saw these people huddled together
against the far wall.
My heart stopped.
I stood still as ice.
The kind of people in a place like this
would kill me for my coat.
Finally I could make out . . .
There was . . . this baby.
This mother and this baby,

19th Day of Advent

I could tell plain it was new born,
being so dry blood smeared and
blue cold looking and wrinkled.
And laying with them a gray bearded man
with his arm around the woman.
They were dozing and didn't see me.
I crept closer and knelt down between the animals.

You could tell from the way place looked
a flock of people like the shepherds,
had been there, churning up muck and straw,
making it all messier than ever,
this filthy place where the animals
stood in a stupor, needing a bath
even more than me.

Could this baby be the Messiah?
I almost laughed out loud.
Some Messiah.
The place stunk, like me.
Maybe worse.
This stable had a stink
that had gathered, layered, ripened
for months, for years.
Dirt, dung, animals' sour breath,
decay, dead things in the cracks,
and me crouching in a corner
in muck and shreds churned up
by shepherds surely no less shameful than I.

19th Day of Advent

It was like all the stink of the world was there
with a Messiah mixed in,
this baby wrapped in rags,
by a mother appearing to be
as wild and drained as the crazy woman,
and an old man who could have been,
not to lie . . . a goatherd
judging from his looks.

If this baby was the Messiah,
which at that moment didn't seem likely,
at least he didn't give people like me,
a stink like mine,
a wide berth.

Sitting there, I started to cry.
I didn't quite know why. Me. Crying.
Like a scream, not knowing
whether from joy or pain or fear or need,
or all of them and more.

It was Keturah's face I saw, then,
through my tears, remembering her,
that tough, toothless hag of an angel.
"Stay watchful," she had warned.
And here I was crying like a baby.
Then I heard words, I don't know from where
except it was a woman's voice, like a lullaby:
"He has scattered the proud
in the thoughts of their hearts . . .
and lifted up the lowly."

19th Day of Advent

My head jerked up.
The mother was looking right at me.
Had she spoken those words?
Her eyes were full of surprise,
as if wondering why I was there,
but smiling, too, she was,
as if to accept me all the same.

"My name is Mary," she said softly.
Nodding, she whispered, "This is Jesus."
That voice. I *had* heard it before.
It was like an echo in my head . . .
"He has scattered the proud . . .
He has lifted up the lowly . . .
lifted up the lowly . . .
lifted up the lowly."

Then the baby was crying.
I heard it plain as a goat bleating.
Then he wasn't crying.
When I looked again
they were all looking at me.
The baby was wide-eyed,
his eyes full of secrets and fire.
The old man's eyes were crinkled
in a kind of smile as if to say
he and I both knew something,
which was that we didn't know.
It was like a dream.
It was like home.

19th Day of Advent

As I sat there, the baby began to look around
like he couldn't figure out where he was either.
It was that look made me think
maybe he really could be the Messiah.
He just accepted it, the strangeness
the place, the stink, me, himself,
without seeming ashamed of any of it,
or having to give any of it a wide berth.
It was the strangest night.
The strangeness changed everything.
I remember it so as to tell 'em.
How could I forget?

Though I don't quite know
when I left the cave
or which direction I went,
somehow I got back that night
with my pigeon walk.
It was like waking from a dream.

What I remembered first
was hearing the goats off in the distance,
and then stumbling over something
as I moved closer to stir the fire
in the final darkness before the dawn.
For safety, you are careful, walking like a pigeon.
You learn each stone and hollow of each camp.
So I do not often stumble.

That night I did.
I reached to grab and throw aside
whatever the cursed thing was
that threw me off my stride.
My God, it was another baby . . .
still smeared with blood like the other one,
but bluer with the cold,
wrapped in the oddly lovely, flimsy white shawl
of the crazy woman!
Keturah had been right:
The crazy woman had been with child.

20th Day of Advent

I searched for the crazy woman in the dark,
a few steps in each direction,
but she was not there.
Why was this baby left here?
What was I to do with it?
Maybe it was as dead as it seemed,
since it didn't move or cry.
But then it opened its eyes
and looked at me, as if it, too,
wondered what I would do.
I shifted the baby to my other arm.
The shawl fell away.
It was a girl.
That settled it!

Ah, but I would have done it anyway,
life being hard enough out here,
there being no room in it for a child,
no way to care for it,
not enough food.
And no one else would take it, raise it either.
All the time, babies, children die
and who cares to ask how they do, or why?
You just get rid of 'em,
especially if they're female,
as this one was.
You leave 'em to die,
in the cold, for the wolves,
like the mother did who left her here
for me to stumble over.

20th Day of Advent

I put the baby down by the fire
and went to check the goats.
They were restless.
One of them, young Zamza,
had given first birth while I was gone.
I found her dead.
Another goat had taken the newborn kid as her own
and was nursing it in the early light.

I began to cry. Not for years had I,
then twice in the same strange night,
I sobbed as if I'd lost something,
or found something, or both.
What was I feeling,
kneeling there in the mud
by the dead mother goat?
I remembered the scream, the crazy woman's scream.
She must have been feeling birth pangs
even as she ran through the night.
Why was that crazy woman
so determined to go to Bethlehem?
Why was I?

I cried and watched the nursing kid
and thought of the Messiah in the stink.
I saw that baby's face, his eyes.
I heard again that voice, that lullaby,
"He has lifted up the lowly . . .
lifted up the lowly . . .
lifted up the lowly."

20th Day of Advent

I got up and walked back to the fire.
I took off my coat and wrapped the baby in it.
I called her, "Mary."
I took the skin from Zamza's body,
cut way and scraped clean her small milk bag
with its virgin pink teat,
and dried it best I could by the fire.
Then I sewed it up, left an opening at the top,
put goat milk in it,
and little Mary nursed at this breast.

So it went for many months,
as me and the goats moved around
in the constant search for pasture.
The goats liked Mary, I could tell.
Then late one afternoon,
Keturah came to visit again.
We sat quiet by the fire
and watched the sun go down.
All she said was,
"I knew you'd take care of her."

Then she handed me the curious thin, white shawl
the crazy woman had worn and I'd found Mary wrapped in
when I stumbled over her that strangest of nights.
I'd thrown it away as a useless rag weeks ago.
"I thought you might like to keep this," Keturah said,
"to give to little Mary someday from her mother."

I didn't ask her how she knew the baby's name,
or how she'd come by the shawl

20th Day of Advent

and mended it to be like it was that strangest of nights.
It was enough that I knew this toothless hag
was some sort of terrible, tender angel,
and that little Mary's mother
had died giving her birth.
The rest was all Keturah's work.

Keturah smiled that toothless smile and said,
"The shepherds are different, too.
It was a wide birth that night."
Then she was gone.

The strangeness of it is all past figuring out.
I started laughing at what Keturah said.
Maybe I was right in my ignorance.
Maybe there is another way to see
what a wide berth means.
Maybe it does mean having a baby.
Giving life to many all around.
So the one born in Bethlehem, that baby Jesus,
does give wide birth, wide life.

That wide birth rippled out to me
so I wasn't so ashamed anymore.
It rippled out to the crazy woman,
who gave birth herself that night.
And to little Mary
because I saved her.
And I did raise her
until she was five years old.

20th Day of Advent

Then Keturah came to visit one last time.
She said, "Mary's of an age to be with a family,
not out here in the wild.
There's a childless couple in Magdala.
I'll take her there."

So I cried a third time.
Both of us cried.
Mary and me.
And Keturah, too.
But it was right for Mary to go with Keturah.
I knew that because I loved her.

That was years ago now.
The strangeness of that night changed everything.
I remember to tell 'em.
Little Mary come to be called Mary Magdalene.
That is how she is known now.
She used to visit me, sometimes.
Then she stopped.
For a time the word was she was a prostitute,
like her mother.

Then little Mary hooked up with Jesus.
Once or twice, I went to see her,
and this Jesus.
I stood at the edge of the crowd
and watched and listened.
She was wearing the shawl I'd found her in,
that strangest of nights.
Little Mary spotted me and came to me both times.

We talked a little, remembered.
Both times she said, "I love you."
And me, stinky old me, managed to choke out,
"I love you, too."

The last time I visited little Mary
she took me to meet Jesus.
I knew it was the same one
I'd met that strangest of all nights.
His eyes held the same secrets and fire.
And he knew too, who I was.
I don't know how, but he did.
All he said to me was, "I love you."

For the fourth time I cried,
and croaked, "I love you, too."
But the words came out like a scream,
of pain and joy and fear and need,
and more, of great gratitude and hope.
Jesus smiled, then, his father's smile,
to let me know, I'm sure,
we both knew a mystery we didn't completely know
but that knew us altogether.

Little Mary visited me the last time not long ago.
They killed Jesus.
Killed him for not being the kind of Messiah
they wanted or expected.
What fools we are.
What shameful fools.
If only they knew what they don't know

20th Day of Advent

but are known by.
Even when I remember and tell 'em,
they don't pay me no mind.
Or him either.
But there's hope for us. Hope.

Little Mary of Magdala said Jesus had come back,
returned from the dead.
She had seen him.
She was following him still.
So the wide birth isn't over yet. Not yet.

> *(TO GOATS, DANCING)*
> *Hey-o, Pildash, Mosa, Samson.*
> *The fire and the secrets in his eyes.*
> *And he's coming again.*
> *Coming again*
> *Coming again.*
> *He lifts up the lowly . . .*
> *lifts up the lowly . . .*
> *lifts up the lowly . . .*

And
Now . . .

Gum on the Altar

hen the chariots of the Lord, rolling out on shafts of light and through timeless darknesses and unknown worlds, break rank to wheel and scatter round planets like our own, finding their way into curious and unlikely corners of such planets — for curious and unlikely reasons, bearing curious and unlikely messages — you might guess there are curious and unlikely creatures in them, hanging on to the reins as much to stay in the chariot as to guide it. Who knows where such messages — and messengers — might end up? So it is well to pay attention!

Consider, if you will, two old women walking to lunch, as snow begins to fall. Could they be . . . ?

"It's snowing, Rose," observed one of the women named Phoebe.

Rose, the other woman, engaged in what truly were her own thoughts, mumbled to herself, "Do you think green would match the trees if I opened the door to sneeze when the gardener squeezed and the air is nice if it's blue as ice but Mrs. Vassick ain't so full of spice and . . ."

"Rose. ROSE!"

"Yes? Oh, Phoebe, it's you. Yes, it is. Yes. What?"

"It's snowing, Rose."

"Well, yes it is," Rose agreed. "It certainly is. Yes, it is. It is snowing. Yes, certainly, it is. It is . . . "

"Rose!"

"Yes? Yes, Phoebe?"

"Rose, I heard no two snowflakes is alike. Not one like another."

"Is that a fact?" exclaimed Rose. "Well now, ain't that something. Just imagine that. Ain't no two snow flakes alike. Ain't that something. Think of . . . How did they find that out, Phoebe?"

"I don't know. I just heard it's so."

"My. Now, ain't they getting smart," said Rose. "They just know everything these days, don't they. Imagine knowing ain't no two snowflakes alike. Imagine knowing these snowflakes we're mashing under our feet right now ain't like no other snowflakes anywhere forever and ever. How do they know that, Phoebe? That no snowflakes ain't like no other snowflakes forever and ever and never and lever and clever and . . . "

"Rose."

"Yes?"

"Rose, how many snowflakes do you think there are?"

"Well, let me see," Rose answered. "A lot! Certainly a lot. Oh, a very lot. A thousand, probably. Oh, more. More than a thousand. A hundred thousand? A thousand thousand? Oh, I know it's a very, very lot. How many, Phoebe?"

"Zillions, Rose. Zillions and trillions and millions."

"Is that a fact, Phoebe? That many. Well, now ain't that something. That is something, ain't it? That certainly is a lot. A very, very lot. A very, very, very . . . "

"Rose!"

"Yes? Yes, Phoebe. Yes. What is it?"

"Who makes snowflakes?" asked Phoebe.

"Who makes snowflakes? Oh, well now . . . let me see. Who makes snowflakes? Who makes . . . let me see. I . . . ah . . . I don't know, Phoebe. I don't know, do I, Phoebe? I should know, but I forgot. I'm going to cry. I am. Going to cry. I don't know. I just forgot."

"Rose! Don't cry, Rose. It's all right. I'll tell you who makes snowflakes. God makes snowflakes, that's who."

"Oh, good for you, Phoebe! You remembered. Good for you. Of course. God makes snowflakes. I forgot. Ain't that something? Of course. Certainly God makes . . . How do they know that, Phoebe?"

"Reverend Thurston says so, in chapel," answered Phoebe. "He says that God makes everything. Remember?"

"Did he say that? Oh, yes. Of course he did. I remember now. Ain't that something. God makes everything. Snowflakes, too. Certainly, of course."

"Besides," confided Phoebe, "last night I heard little voices and they kept saying, 'God made us, God made us.' Over and over. And I looked all around, and it was the snowflakes talking through the window. Did you hear 'em?"

But Rose was off in her own thoughts again, talking to herself. "Coke is good. I like Coke, and I don't smoke or tell no jokes and old cow pokes and . . . why don't they let me have Cokes? Is two small Cokes more than one big Coke? I asked the man, but he said I didn't have enough money. Two cents, I had. Change. Home on the range. Where everything's strange . . . "

"ROSE! Listen to me, Rose."

"Oh, Phoebe? It's you. Yes. Certainly. I was listening. Yes, I certainly was. I was, yes, I was, and . . . and you was talking about . . . about . . ."

"Snowflakes, Rose."

"Yes. That's it. Good for you, Phoebe! You remembered. Good for you. That's it. We was talking about snowflakes. Of course. Certainly. Phoebe, you look sort of sick. What's the matter, dear?"

21st Day of Advent

"Rose, I ain't sick. Now just shut up a minute. I'm just thinking, is all. Rose, if God makes snowflakes, and no two snowflakes is alike, and there are zillions and trillions of snowflakes, God must be terrible busy. So how does God have time to do much else but make snowflakes?"

"How does God have time to do . . . oh my," Rose struggled. "That's a hard one. Let me see. I should know the answer to that, shouldn't I? Let me see . . . Maybe snowflakes . . . Maybe snowflakes . . . Maybe God . . . I can't remember. I'm going to cry, Phoebe. I'm just going to cry."

"Don't cry, Rose. It's all right. Maybe they'll let you have a Coke for lunch."

Two women, curious and unlikely creatures, on their way to lunch as the snow falls in a curious and unlikely corner of the planet — The State Mental Hospital — where they are for curious and unlikely reasons, though perhaps no more curious and unlikely than any of us curious and unlikely creatures are, wherever it is that we are.

The last of the many jobs Phoebe did to support her invalid mother was selling hot dogs and soda as a street vendor. Her cart was mounted on a three-wheel bicycle she rode about town. When her mother died, Phoebe kept riding her cart, selling her hot dogs and listening to the voices she'd begun to hear about a year before.

One evening she'd ridden her cart to a corner near the Symphony Hall where stylishly dressed people had to walk around her while she hawked her wares. When a policeman told her to move, she argued that she wouldn't because stronger voices than his had told her to come to that particular corner on that particular night, and she wouldn't move.

"Thank you very much, get lost Buddy Boy!"

The argument got heated, the policeman threatened to arrest

her, and Phoebe began throwing paper cups and hot-dog wrappers around on the sidewalk, followed by buns and hot dogs. A crowd gathered. When the embarrassed policeman took Phoebe by the arm to lead her away, she kicked him and threw soda on his uniform. He called a wagon and they picked her up bodily and carted her away.

After a night in jail, the court committed Phoebe to The State Mental Hospital for psychiatric tests. The tests were legally inconclusive, but since she had no family or outside advocate, her case got conveniently buried. So the women's geriatric ward became home for Phoebe.

Her friend Rose had been married. Her one child, a son, had run off to join the Merchant Marine at seventeen and had not been heard from again. Rose's heart was broken. After her husband died, she'd ended up living alone in a small apartment on his pension. At first she had a cat to talk to, but after a while she'd begun talking not only to the cat but to herself. Slowly she seemed to lose track of things, including the thread of her own conversations.

Then one winter evening a policeman had found her shivering on a street corner, talking rapidly in what seemed to him an irrational and incoherent way. They held her in the Women's Detention Center for several weeks, but tracing her through missing persons turned up nothing, and Rose simply couldn't remember where she lived or anyone she knew. So after much indecision, someone in the Welfare Department suggested The State Mental Hospital and, thus nudged into the bureaucratic maze, Rose found her way at last to the women's geriatric ward and the bed next to Phoebe's.

Two women, curious and unlikely creatures, side-by-side in a curious and unlikely corner of the planet. Though perhaps they are no more curious and unlikely than any of us curious and unlikely creatures are, side-by-side, wherever it is that we are in our corner of the planet.

Phoebe and Rose had become inseparable. One was round, the other bony. One shuffled along, the other swayed in a bow-legged way. One talked to herself, the other heard voices. Neither could put into words how they felt about the other, and it did not occur to them to try. They didn't even think about it. They were simply inseparable.

"Here's the dining room, Rose," said Phoebe. "Give me your arm for the steps."

"Orange is nice, all sticky and spice, icky as mice, ran up the clock, hickory dock, cat on the block, which one is right, right is nice, nice is bright, bright is nice, nice is . . .," Rose rambled on.

"Rose."

"Yes? Oh, Phoebe. It's you. I was listening, I certainly was. Certainly, yes, listening I was. I was, really, I . . ."

"Here is the dining room," instructed Phoebe. "Give me your arm for the steps."

"Oh yes! Good, good, good. Time for lunch. Thanks a bunch. Do you think I can have a Coke? Phoebe, do you think I can have a Coke? For lunch? Do you? Do you think I can, do you, do you, do you?"

"Maybe," replied Phoebe. "Maybe you can have a Coke, and I can get some gum. Got a quarter in my pocket. For the gum machine. Pull the lever; it says, 'Thank you!' Do you hear it say that, Rose? Pull the lever; it says, 'Thank you. Here comes the gum. Thank you! Thank you!' Do you hear it, Rose?"

One loved Coke, the other loved gum. Curious and unlikely! Though Phoebe didn't have many teeth left, she loved to chew gum, though chewing was only *one* thing she did with gum — perhaps the least of the things she did with it. She sucked on it, gummed it, rolled it around in her mouth, swallowed it, blew bubbles with it (if it was bubble gum, getting it all over her face), pulled it out of her mouth in long strings, put it behind her ear sometimes where it usually got stuck in her hair.

Worst of all, she would leave wads of chewed gum every place. Many of the places she left it, and forgot about it, were harmless enough. Often she would leave it on her little bed stand overnight and chew it again the next day, marveling at how hard it got during the night, and how she could see her tooth marks in it just as she'd left it when she'd gone to bed. But other places she left her gum were more troublesome.

Phoebe and Rose worked in the hospital laundry together, Rose folding towels, Phoebe folding sheets. Many times Phoebe had left her used gum next to a pile of just-washed sheets before they were rolled through the big mangle irons. Often her gum ended up sticking on the sheets when they rolled through the mangles, and the resulting mess caused furor after furor until, finally the laundry supervisor simply forbade her to chew gum, which, for the most part she didn't, while she worked.

Still, her gum also caused problems when she accidentally left it where people sat, or walked. To top everything, when Reverend Thurston came, once a month, to give Holy Communion in the chapel over the dining room in her building, Phoebe would invariably go forward with the others to receive the elements, only to remember her gum just as the bread was being passed. So, just as invariably, she would remove her gum and put it, only for a moment she thought, on the communion rail while she chewed the bread, thinking it would be terrible to mix her chewing gum with the "Body of Christ."

But, invariably, Phoebe forgot about her gum and left it behind when she returned to her pew. So, regularly, Reverend

22nd Day of Advent

Thurston stopped by the ward on his way back to his church and gave her a little talk about good manners in worship, which meant, specifically, that she should not chew gum in the chapel. She was never sure exactly what he was saying, or why, but each time, she agreed not to chew during worship, only to forget her agreement by the time the next month's communion came around.

Recently, Reverend Thurston had approached her again about the gum she'd left on the rail during the Advent communion service.

"Phoebe," Reverend Thurston admonished, "you put your gum on the communion rail again. You simply must stop doing that. It is irreverent, it is offensive to God, and it desecrates a holy place."

"I'm sorry, Reverend," Phoebe answered. "I just forget. I don't mean no harm, really. What does 'desecrate' mean?"

"It means . . . well . . ." Thurston groped for words to explain what it never occurred to him needed explaining. "It means to take something clean and make it dirty. Phoebe, how would you like it if someone took your clean sheets and got them all dirty after you washed and folded them? Well, that's how God feels about gum on the communion rail."

"But, Reverend, ain't people supposed to get sheets dirty? If you use 'em, how can you keep from getting 'em dirty? That's why we wash 'em. I don't understand about desecrate."

"Well," stammered Thurston, feeling flustered, "desecrate is, well . . . it's . . . it's taking something that's supposed to be used one way, the right way, and using it another way, the wrong way. That's what desecrate means. Using something wrongly, for what it wasn't intended to be used for. You see what I mean, Phoebe?" He felt pleased with himself.

22nd Day of Advent

"I think so," Phoebe nodded, smiling. "It's like Jesus being born in a stable, like you read in the Bible to us. That's using the stable for another way than was meant, right? Jesus desecrated the stable. Is that sorta what you mean?"

"No, that is not at all what I mean." Thurston's face contorted between anger and foolishness. "Phoebe, you are deliberately refusing to see my point."

"I ain't trying to miss it, Reverend. Really. I'll . . . I'll remember next time not to chew gum. Don't worry, Reverend."

"Good." Thurston was relieved to leave the subject of desecration. "Just think how other people feel, seeing your gum on the rail when they come to the Lord's Table, Phoebe. Try to remember next time." He turned to leave.

"Excuse me, Reverend, but . . . I been wondering about them wise men, you know, the ones you read about? Why did they bring them gifts to baby Jesus?"

"To honor him as King and Deity," answered Reverend Thurston, turning back.

"But what is franka . . . franka . . . "

"Frankincense, Phoebe? It is like incense. It smells good. It's used to worship the Deity. It means Jesus is Lord."

"Oh. And what about the other stuff they brung? Not the gold. The other stuff. You know."

"Yes, myrrh. That is like a rare resin, Phoebe."

"Resin? What's that?"

"Well, it's like a kind of gummy substance," replied Reverend Thurston.

Phoebe brightened. "Gummy? Like gum?"

"Not *gum* gum, Phoebe. It's more like . . . well, they use it to make perfume and to make a liquid they used to bury people with in ancient times."

22nd Day of Advent

"Oh. Bury people? Ain't that a stupid thing to bring a little baby, Reverend?"

"It's symbolic, Phoebe. They brought it because they knew Jesus would die for the sins of the world. As it says in the Bible, in Revelation, 'Worthy is the Lamb who was slain, to receive power and wealth and wisdom and might and honor and glory and blessing.' It's symbolic, the myrrh."

"A lamb, Reverend? I don't get it."

"Well, Phoebe, that's symbolic, too. A lamb is a symbol of innocence, you see. A little lamb is innocent. And Jesus was innocent. An innocent sacrifice is acceptable to God. Because of it, God forgives our sins."

"Sort of like Jesus helps us and helps God," Phoebe mused.

"In a manner of speaking," Thurston replied.

"And that's what myrrh means?" she asked.

"That is what it means. Or close enough for you. Now, I have to go. Just remember, Phoebe, no more gum in the chapel." He sighed as he walked away.

Phoebe didn't understand what Reverend Thurston was saying, but probably he didn't either, though his departing sigh was as close as he'd ever come to admitting it, even to himself. So the difference was that she was troubled by not understanding and he wasn't. She struggled to understand because she knew she didn't; and he didn't struggle to understand because he thought he did.

And that is how messages get missed — curious and unlikely messages from curious and unlikely creatures hanging on for dear life to the reins of the Lord's chariot wheeling in curious and unlikely places.

22nd Day of Advent

Another curious thing about this curious place was that many of the buildings of The State Mental Hospital were connected by underground tunnels that were used for walkways as well as passages for plumbing and heating lines. It was an old building, built before electricity or inside plumbing or central heating. So when each of these conveniences was added, all sorts of conduits and pipes were attached to the walls. When you entered the building, you felt a little like Jonah in the belly of the whale, watching and listening to its vital juices pass through its tracts and ducts and glands. Rumor had it that the old building was to be torn down soon and another built to replace it.

In fact, much of the life of the hospital took place in those tunnels and in the veritable warren of storage rooms and closets running off them. The dining room of Phoebe's and Rose's unit was on the first floor in the center of a two-story building. The chapel was over the dining room on the second floor, so, "symbolically," God and the kitchen held together the women's geriatric ward in the east wing and the men's geriatric ward in the west wing.

It was into the belly of this whale that Rose and Phoebe made their way to lunch. They had just come to their table and sat down when Dr. Kaplan announced that the Trinity Church youth choir would be singing Christmas carols for them that noon, and the auxiliary of the local Rotary Club would pass out gifts. The gifts turned out to be a box of Kleenex and a bag of candy for everyone. Phoebe gladly noted that the bag of candy had a package of gum in it. Suddenly overwhelmed by the prospect, she began to cry.

And no sooner than the choir began to sing, Rose began to talk: "Trick or treat, kiss my feet. Wear your rubbers, oh yes,

23rd Day of Advent

mother. Bundle up, you'll catch your death, look at there, you can see your breath. Johnny's all dead and gone. Everybody sing a song. Red is dead and so's the brain inside your head, and so is Fred with dirty feet . . . "

"Rose, shhh," whispered Phoebe, "they're singing . . ."

Rose blithely babbled on, "Freddy stinks and Mary winks and Daddy drinks. But I won't tell, so what the . . ."

"Rose, Rose, shhh. They're singing. SHHHHHHHHH. ROSE."

"Yes? Oh, Phoebe. It's you. I was listening. Really. I was . . . Oh, Phoebe, you're crying. Oh, don't cry. Please, don't cry. What's the matter? Oh, I'm going to cry, too. Oh, Phoebe, Phoebe."

"Shhh, Rose. I'm just feeling a little bad 'cause people give us things, and I ain't got nothing to give nobody. Not even you, Rose. Nothing to give for Christmas."

"Ahh, Phoebe, you're my friend. You give me you. Best thing anybody could have. You're my friend. Don't feel bad, please. You're the nicest friend anybody ever had. Don't cry, Phoebe, please don't."

"Shhh. Rose, be quiet. Listen to the music now. Stop talking and listen. Shhh."

Rose turned to listen, and Phoebe looked at her a long time, thinking about what she had said, until the choir finished and everyone was clapping. An idea had begun to form in her mind.

Since the snow continued to fall, Phoebe and Rose and most of the other patients used the tunnels to return to their afternoon activities. On their way back, the group stopped and gathered in a large storage room where several mattresses had been put on the floor and an old record player stood in one corner. At odd hours, especially at night, patients would sneak down to this room for little parties and social liaisons, all officially forbidden but unofficially

23rd Day of Advent

sanctioned by the hospital authorities. Such activities obviously helped patient morale and so helped the hospital run more smoothly. And on this particular day, many in the little gathering were grumbling about the gift of Kleenex and wishing some group would give them some beer sometime, or something for a party.

But while they grumbled, Phoebe was busy trading her candy to women for their gum and giving kisses and other small favors, along with the promises of future considerations, for the men's gum. By the time she returned to the laundry, she had eighty-seven packages of gum and promises of at least twenty-three more. That night she also counted her little savings, slowly dividing it into little piles, each of which would buy one package of gum; she determined she'd be able to buy another thirty-four packages, maybe more.

During the following week, though no one really noticed, Phoebe left no wads of chewing gum anywhere. And every night, late into the night, Phoebe sat on the edge of her bed chewing stick after stick of gum until her jaws ached.

"Phoebe, what are you doing?" asked Rose sleepily on her midnight return from the bathroom.

"Chewing gum, can't you see?" Phoebe sighed. "Just go to sleep, Rose. Don't worry."

"Why are you chewing all your gum like that, Phoebe? Why don't you save it? You're using it all up. Why are you doing that?"

"I'm making something is why. For Christmas."

"What, Phoebe? What are you making? Something for me? For me, Phoebe? For me?"

"Not exactly for you, Rose. It's a . . . surprise. It's mainly for God."

"God? You're making something for God? Ain't that something. For God. That's something, Phoebe. It certainly is. It is, certainly. How did you know what God wants, Phoebe?"

"I don't know. I just . . . I don't know."

"Surprise. For God. Ain't that something. Phoebe, you said that God made snowflakes, but I forgot what else you said. About snowflakes. What'd you say?"

"That I heard 'em talking?" answered Phoebe.

"That's it. Good for you, Phoebe! You remembered. That's what you said, all right. You heard 'em talking. You certainly did. How come I don't hear 'em, Phoebe?"

"You're too busy talking," Phoebe replied.

"Oh. I never thought of that. What do they say, Phoebe? The snowflakes. What do they say?"

" 'God made us. God made us.' That's what they say, Rose. And Rose, no two snowflakes is alike, remember?"

"That's right," said Rose. "That's what you said. I remember now. And you said there was zillions and zillions of 'em. See, I was listening, Phoebe. I was. How many is a zillion, Phoebe?"

"A lot," Phoebe answered. "A very, very lot, as you say."

"Oh. Why was we talking about that, Phoebe?"

"'Cause I was wondering, if God made all them snowflakes, how does God have time to do anything else? Answer me that, Rose."

"Oh. OHHHHH. I forgot what you said. Let me see . . . I forgot. I . . . I think I'm going to cry. Phoebe. Yes, I am. I'm going to cry."

"It's all right, Rose. Don't cry. I don't know either. God must be pretty busy. So . . . so I'm making God a little surprise. Now go to sleep."

During that week, Phoebe chewed one hundred thirty-seven packages of gum. She used all the money she had saved to buy more, and she begged from doctors and nurses and attendants, and traded with other patients, and even took some from the commissary when the clerk wasn't looking. And every night she chewed. By the week before Christmas she had asked Rose to help her.

"But I don't like to chew gum, Phoebe," said Rose. "I just ain't got no good teeth."

"You gotta help, Rose. Or I won't finish my surprise in time for Christmas."

"But I can't talk good when I chew gum. The gum sticks to my teeth. See, ah caahhn't tahhk gahhd."

"You don't have to talk," said Phoebe. "Just chew and chew and chew, Rose. Rose? Rose did you hear something just then?"

"Ahhh, naaw. Ahh dahhn't heaah nahhthin."

"Shhh. Listen. It's singing, Rose. Singing. You hear it?"

"Naaw, nahhthin. Ahh daahhn't heaah nahh sahhing."

"Chew, Rose. Chew faster. The angels is coming. Already. Listen. That's them singing. Oh, hurry up. Hurry."

So the night before Christmas Eve, Rose and Phoebe sat on their beds across from each other and chewed the last packages of Phoebe's hoard of gum. When they had finished, they gathered the fresh wads of chewed gum, snuck out past the night attendant who was asleep in the little glass-enclosed office, and went downstairs into the basement. They made their way along the dimly-lit tunnel to a small closet off one of the storage rooms. Phoebe lit a candle she had hidden there.

"See, Rose. That's what I been making," said Phoebe. "That's where the gum I been chewing went. See. What do you think?"

"Why, that's the biggest wad of chewed up gum I ever seen, Phoebe. Ain't that something. It certainly is. It certainly is something, ain't it? You been making that? It's something. What is it, Phoebe?"

"It's a statue, Rose, can't you tell? Here, I'll pick it up so you can see. See, the gum got all hard when I stuck it together. Now, what do you think?"

"Let me see," answered Rose, "I should know what that is. It's . . . it's chewing gum, that's a fact, ain't it? Chewing gum all chewed up, little clumps stuck together in a statue of . . . of . . . of . . . a cat? That's it. A cat! It's a cat is what it is. Like my cat. Emily cat. Nice cat. Orange cat. Orange peel, real meal, happy deal . . . "

"Rose. ROSE!"

"Yes, Phoebe?"

"It's not no cat," said Phoebe. "It's a lamb. Can't you see the wool? Curly all over it. Now, this gum we chewed tonight is for one ear and a little tail. Stick some on right there, and . . . there. Like that. Squeeze it a little. There. Good. That will be hard in the morning. And see there, his legs bent under him, 'cause he's lying down. And this here's the nose. Could of been a little longer, maybe, but I run outta gum. It's a lamb, Rose."

"Good for you, Phoebe! You knew right off it was a lamb. Of course. It certainly is. That's what it is. A lamb. Yes, that's what it is, all right. What are you going to do with it, Phoebe?"

"Put it on the altar. In the chapel. For God."

"Does God chew gum, Phoebe? How did you know that? I didn't know that. Now ain't that something. Certainly is. It certainly is something that you knew . . ."

"NOT TO CHEW, ROSE! It's like, how did Reverend say it, it's 'symbotic.' That's it. 'Symbotic.' Gum is what I love. So this lamb is symbotic of me, of my love. So it'll be like me, on the altar. You see, like Jesus was symbotic of the lamb. Or the lamb was symbotic. I ain't too clear on that. But I just thought, since God's got so much to do, with the snowflakes and everything, and . . . I ain't got much. But . . . to cheer God up and help out, I'd give this . . . symbotic . . . gum lamb . . . of my love . . . or something like that."

23rd Day of Advent

Befuddled, Rose returned to her own thoughts and conversation. "Coke is good. Are two small Cokes more than one big one? But too much ice is not too nice. Slip on ice, slide on snow. Go and blow and stop the show."

"Rose!"

"Phoebe? It is you. I was listening. I was. I certainly was. I just got thirsty is what happened. Can we get a Coke, please. Can we? Please?"

"Rose. Rose. Dear, Rose. Come on. I got a quarter. We'll sneak down to the dining room machine." Sneak? No! One shuffled, the other swayed through the tunnel of The State Mental Hospital to the Coke machine in the dining room, then back to the women's geriatric ward and bed. Curious unlikely creatures in a curious unlikely place for curious unlikely reasons.

Then it was Christmas Eve, that holiest of times. After the lights were out, Phoebe and Rose snuck out again. It was easier this time, since most of the attendants were off. Down they went to the basement, into the tunnel, on to the little closet where Phoebe picked up her chewing gum lamb which, crude though it was, bore a striking resemblance to a real lamb, since the wads of gum did look surprisingly like tufts of wool. Then slowly the two friends made their way to the dining room and on up to the chapel above.

The chapel was plain, the floor wooden and creaky. The big windows were of clear glass through which, this night, came the soft light of a full moon. The pulpit was on one side of the small platform, the lectern on the other, as Thurston had properly arranged them. The altar was on the wall to the rear, and on it were two candles and a cross. A dark curtain ran halfway up the wall, and a tiny window, much like a porthole, or a Cyclopean eye, was near the top. In front of the platform was the communion rail. The pews sagged, which gave them a tired look, and there was a musty smell about the place. And it was very warm, warmer even than it usually is in a state building for old people. The two women stood timidly at the back, near the door.

"Shhh," whispered Phoebe.

"Shhh?" asked Rose. "Why? Somebody sleeping in here?"

"No. Ain't no service now. Just don't want nobody to hear us."

"Why? What are you going to do, Phoebe?" asked Rose.

"I ain't exactly sure. Say something, Rose. Something religious. You know. Anything."

"Religious? Something religious. Let me see. I should know something. I . . . Oh, yes. 'The Lord is my shepherd. I shall not' . . . not . . . ahh . . . shall not . . ."

24th Day of Advent

"Want, Rose. Want."

"Want what, Phoebe? What?"

"Nothing, Rose. Just, 'I shall not want.' 'Want' is what you couldn't think of. 'The Lord is my shepherd, I shall not want.' "

"Don't be cross, Phoebe. I just forgot. I forgot. I . . . I'm going to cry. I don't think I like it in here alone like this."

"You ain't alone, Rose. I'm here. Now come on! I'll just put my lamb on the altar and we'll go. Come on."

"Phoebe, I don't like sneaking around like this. Don't like sneaking. Don't like creaking. Yellow's bad but black is sad and green is seen beneath the dream . . . "

"Shhh, Rose! Do you hear something?"

". . . beyond the scheme, the trees are bare, there's no cat hair, the night is spare, there is nowhere . . . "

"Rose! ROSE!"

"Yes? Oh, Phoebe. Yes, I'm listening. I am. I certainly am."

"Do you hear something, Rose? Do you? High, like music?"

"Do I hear . . . music? Do you? What is it, Phoebe? Why can't I hear it?"

"Listen. Listen. Where is it? Voices. Where are they coming from? Where? Where? Come on, Rose. We got to follow 'em. Come on."

They left the chapel and stood in the hallway, listening. To their left were the big wooden doors leading to the women's ward, second floor, and to their right, the same kind of doors leading to the second floor of the men's ward. Those doors were kept locked and looked formidable. But from behind the doors on the men's side came the sound of voices, weak but panicked voices, moans and screams without much volume, as from old men, sick, tired, confused. What looked like smoke was coming from under the doors.

24th Day of Advent

"Look, Phoebe. Look. Look," cried Rose.

"I see. I see. Come on. Quick, quick."

As fast as they could, they moved down the hall and began pushing on the doors.

"Push, Rose. Push. Push," yelled Phoebe. "As hard as you can. Push."

"I am. I am, Phoebe. As hard as I can."

Big as the doors looked, they were old and had been ignored for years.

Their locks were old-fashioned, too, and gave way rather easily. The women pushed into the men's ward. It was full of steam — hot, live steam that made it hard to see and harder to breathe. Side gates were up on most beds, and many men were unable to get out of them without help. They were gasping, coughing. Those closest to the leaking steam pipe were being scalded as the steam gushed out from the pipe where it ran along the wall two- or three-feet off the floor. The pipes were unusually large because they not only carried steam for the entire wing, but also went from the heating plant, through this building, down into the tunnel, and on to three more buildings,

"We got to help these men get out, Rose," shouted Phoebe. "Through the doors. Quick, quick."

Somehow Rose and Phoebe were rejuvenated rather than panicked by the crisis. Coughing, they edged into the room, reaching the first men.

"I can't . . . see too good . . . Phoebe," Rose sputtered, reaching to take one of the old men's hands, then saying to him, "Here, this way . . . this way. Come on . . . that's it. Climb out . . . over the end. Never mind those bars . . . Come on . . . Phoebe . . . Phoebe, where are you?"

Phoebe was crawling along, pushing her lamb ahead of her

and toward the hissing sound, following it to its source. The steam hissed and roared, tore at her lungs, clawed at her face, scalded her flesh, and seared her eyes whenever she opened them. Finally, she stood, held her gum lamb in front of her, and pushed it with all of her strength at the hissing sound. Slowly the sound muffled. She pushed harder. The steam dissipated slightly. With her hands she could feel where the joint had pulled loose. The heat softened the gum. As best she could, she stuffed it around the leaking wound in the pipe. Then she turned to help the man in the nearest bed. He was moaning. She tried to push the bed down the aisle toward the door. She couldn't see very well. Her eyes were swollen nearly shut. The pain came with a roar and then a yawning silence. She fell into a merciful blackness.

The next thing she knew, she was lying on her back and someone was holding something to her face, telling her to breathe. It hurt to breathe. She squinted into the light. Rose was holding her hand and crying, "Oh, Phoebe. Oh, Phoebe."

Phoebe could hear something way off. Was it a siren? Or music? She lifted her head, listening. A voice spoke: "Easy. Just take it easy."

She peered as best she could through her swollen lids and could just make out that she was in the chapel, up near the altar. People were moving around. They were all in white, like angels. Other people were lying in the nearby pews.

She could see another person in white, bending over her, looking at her with a bright light, talking in a deep voice to someone she couldn't see: "Some pretty bad burns here. Luckily, everyone got out alive. This woman is the worst. She's burned pretty bad. The word is that she helped save the others. I don't know what she used, but apparently she managed to stop the steam long enough for everyone to get out."

24th Day of Advent

Phoebe pushed the oxygen mask away. She spoke hoarsely, "It was my gum lamb."

"Take it easy, ma'am," the voice said tenderly. Then to the unseen person, it asked more loudly, "What did she say?"

Another voice replied, "I didn't catch it."

"Her gum lamb," replied Rose. "That's what she done. Put her gum lamb on that busted pipe. Ain't that something? Oh, Phoebe. You got to be all right. You got to be. You hear me? You will be, won't you?"

Phoebe smiled and nodded. She had given what was 'symbotic' of her love where it was needed. She didn't understand it all, but she was pretty sure God would. In spite of what the Reverend had said to her, she believed what she'd done was a desecration, sort of like the baby Jesus in the stable. Like it, but different. Like snowflakes are alike, but different. She'd helped a little. She lifted her head again, and listened.

"Do you hear something, Rose," she rasped. "That music, do you hear it?"

"Music? Well . . . maybe I do. Yes, I think I do, Phoebe. Ain't that something? I do. I certainly do. I hear it, Phoebe. Really I do. I do hear it."

Ah yes, that music, do you hear it? Before you answer, you will do well to remember who really asks. For when the chariots of the Lord roll out on shafts of light and through timeless darkness, and break rank to wheel around planets such as our own, finding their way to curious and unlikely corners of it, for curious and unlikely reasons, bearing curious and unlikely messages, embodied in curious and unlikely creatures such as . . . well, who knows? Things are wilder by far than we think and more wondrous than we may yet have dared to believe. Do you hear the music?

24th Day of Advent

"For you shall go out in joy and be led forth in peace; the mountains and the hills before you shall break forth into singing, and all the trees of the field shall clap their hands."[*]

24th Day of Advent

A Personal Epilogue

"Christmas in the Ruins"

One way or another, I always seem to ruin Christmas before it arrives. In committing the ugly deed, I have the usual accomplices everyone recognizes — the relentless rush and commercialism of the season, the depressing idealization and impossible expectations that gild the holiday, the pernicious mix of adrenaline and exhaustion. But when it comes down to it, I also manage to put my own fingerprints on the ruining. Each year I swear it will be different and strain to make it so. And yet . . .

I recall the year my wife Jan and I scheduled a dinner for friends a week or so before Christmas. On the morning of the party, we admitted to each other that we were too tired and pre-occupied to enjoy it, and we fleetingly considered canceling out, but didn't. When our guests arrived, they hinted at having similar feelings. Apparently we'd all "pressed on" out of a sense of social obligation.

Not surprisingly, during the course of the evening the conversation got a bit heated. It was on some topic so important I can't remember it now. Whatever it was, it was laced with a lot of "men *always*, women *never*" comments that tie everyone in a knot of irritation and frustration. The party limped to a close in a mode of sulky civility. No one wanted to prolong the evening by trying to repair the breach we all felt.

When the guests finally left, my accumulated anger hung around like a vampire looking for blood to suck wherever it could

Christmas Day

be found. "Up on the house top, carp, carp, carp . . . down through the chimney, blame, blame, blame." I picked fights with whoever approached, which happened to be Jan and Smidgeon, our dog. Not only was I angry, I was *righteously* angry. I was not one of those "men *never*" types I'd been lumped with.

Like most righteous anger, mine had disastrous consequences. I was helping to clean up the kitchen as I prosecuted my case to an imaginary jury who nodded their heads in agreement with my every word. In the process of ranting and raving, I broke the handle off an old, flower-gilded, gold-rimmed pitcher that had been given to Jan by her beloved, departed grandmother.

I don't know if it was rage or despair, or a misguided impulse of self-justification, or a fit of perversity, but rather than apologize or examine the pitcher to see if it could be repaired, I hurled it to the floor. It smashed into a thousand pieces, the shards and splinters skittering through the kitchen, into the two adjoining rooms and down the stairs to the basement.

Tears filled Jan's eyes as she picked up a piece of the pitcher and held it in her hand. Then she looked at me and whispered, "It's too bad." Without another word, she left the kitchen. I listened to her climb the stairs and walk slowly to our bedroom.

I stood in the ache of silence and felt tears trickle down my cheeks as I realized I'd blown it again. Now it was too late for Christmas to be different this year. And, until that night, I'd been trying so hard! It occurred to me that maybe trying so hard to make it different was part of my problem. I leaned against the kitchen counter and stared at the pieces of porcelain lying on the floor, casualties of some strange warfare in me. Why wasn't I as good as I wanted to be?

I don't know how long I stood there, but my self-examination was interrupted by the sound of Jan's footsteps coming back down

Christmas Day

the stairs to the kitchen. Without a sideward glance, she got out the broom and dustpan, and in silence we began to sweep up the broken pitcher. I could not find words for my shame. It seemed pitiful to say, "I'm sorry," but I did, and Jan said, "I know." For what seemed a very long time, the only other sounds were Smidgeon's sympathetic whimpering, the swish of the broom, and the clinking of the porcelain being swept, picked up, and dropped in a trash bag.

Regret and remorse kept me awake most of the night. In the morning, Jan assured me of her forgiveness, for which I was grateful. Yet I knew her grandmother's cherished pitcher was no more, and worse, something had been broken in her granddaughter's heart. I also knew the breaking was typical of me. I felt a dull, lingering ache.

For the remaining days leading up to Christmas, I kept finding fragments and splinters of that shattered pitcher in strange places. I kept finding them even though I thought I'd found them all several times. I kept finding them in out-of-the-way corners when the light hit them just so — between the counter and the stove, under a chair, in the fold of a jacket hanging on a hook near the door, in small cracks in the wooden floor, behind a rubber boot, under the base of the telephone, on different risers of the basement stairs.

Each time I found another piece of that pitcher, I thought about how much it had meant to Jan, how it had been filled not only with water but with many memories, and much love, and all the hopes that immigrant grandmother had for her granddaughter. I wondered if her grandmother had purchased it at a secondhand store for some of the few pennies she'd saved from her work as a seamstress making buttonholes for suits sold at a large department store in the city. Whatever its story, this vessel of a grandmother's

Christmas Day

love was an accurate, priceless gift to Jan. I often thought about the piece Jan put on her dresser that night when I broke it.

I found what may have been the last piece of that pitcher before going to bed early Christmas morning, after coming home from the midnight Christmas Eve Communion Service. Maybe it had fallen out of the trash bag, but however it got there, the small piece was lying on the driveway just where it intersected with the back alley. I found it because the light of the moon, or the stars, or neighbors' window, hit it just so.

It came to me then that maybe Christmas is like finding those pieces in curious places after the shattering happens. Finding little pieces and slivers of what Christmas means, of what the gift is, in the corners of our lives, in the cracks of our failures and ruinations, down the steps of defeats, and yet, in friends' small expressions of love and forgiveness and trust, in the chances to begin again, and again. Alleys and starlight. God here and there and everywhere. The light penetrating the darkness and hitting just so, unexpectedly, off what is broken and somehow mysteriously reflecting hope.

I picked up the broken piece from the driveway and held it as I walked to the back door, somewhere between Christmas Eve and Christmas morn. I remembered again a grandmother, a granddaughter, and then another woman who long ago had been in painful labor on this night and a child born in an out-of-the-way place, an accurate gift. God there, here, working in a broken world amidst broken people who break things. For the first time, I realized that Christmas isn't about anyone *making* it different. It's about our being aware that it *really is* different, more different than we dare to hope.

I went into the house, through the kitchen, up the stairs and into the bedroom. I put the piece of the pitcher I'd found next to the piece Jan kept on her dresser. This little thing, this token, no

Christmas Day

matter where it had come from, was truly a gift, reminding me that I hadn't really ruined Christmas — I had found it. Or, more's the truth, Christmas had found me.

Christmas Day

DR. THEODORE W. LODER
is the imaginative and socially active
Senior Minister of one of Philadelphia's
most unusual churches, The First United
Methodist Church of Germantown — a
thriving, ethnically-mixed metropolitan
congregation of about one thousand
members. Loder leads this dynamic
church to the forefront of artistic endeav-
ors, political activism, and social justice. His congregation established
a major medical mission in an economically depressed area of the city,
has been a Public Sanctuary Church, a founding church of the Covenant
Against Apartheid in South Africa, and a Reconciling Congregation that
advocates for the rights of homosexual persons. In addition, the church
has a mission project in Guatemala, works with a peasant association in
Fondwa, Haiti, and supports a "For the Love of Children" (FLOC)
Pre-School Program in Johannesburg, South Africa.

Dr. Loder's own social action grows out of a long history of
involvement in social issues, including marching with Dr. Martin Luther
King, Jr., in the sixties; co-founding Metropolitan Career Center (a
job-training program for high school dropouts; co-founding Plowshares
(a non-profit housing renovation corporation); and co-founding Urban
Resource Development Corporation (an ecumenical effort to rehabilitate
abandoned houses). Since 1994, he has also served on the Philadelphia
Mayor's Advisory Commission of Children and Families.

Described as "free-wheeling" and "provocative," "outrageous"
and "emotional," Loder is a breath of fresh air for many people who have
given up on the church. He is widely sought as a preacher and teacher.
His blend of scholarship (cum laude degree from Yale Divinity School,
a university fellow of the Yale Graduate School, and an honorary
doctorate from Willamette University) and creativity (named by the
National Observer as one of America's Outstanding Creative Preachers)
stimulate a refreshing openness to hard questions, to change, to rele-
vance, to justice, to joy.

More Ted Loder Classics

The Haunt of Grace: Responses to the Mystery of God's Presence
192 pages, 0-8066-9034-8

From the pen of one of today's most visionary spiritual thinkers comes a book of profound explorations on the mysteries and marvels of faith, love, and life. In fourteen chapters crafted from his best-loved sermons, Loder's persistently evocative images call us to live in this scarred, beautiful world differently, to find a truer, more compassionate place in it.

My Heart in My Mouth: Prayers for Our Lives
160 pages, 0-8066-9032-1

Loder's gutsy, grace-filled prayers break out of all formulas into heartfelt, mind-opening, soul-searching ways of reaching to God.

Wrestling the Light: Ache and Awe in the Human-Divine Struggle
190 pages, 0-8066-9039-9

Loder gives expression to the depths and joys of the human struggle in these intensely personal prayers,
complimented by six powerful stories.

Available wherever books are sold.